Date Due

LETTERS OF

LOUISE IMOGEN GUINEY

LOUISE IMOGEN GUINEY

FROM A PHOTOGRAPH TAKEN IN CAMBRIDGE, MASS., JUNE 8, 1887
AGED TWENTY-SIX

LETTERS OF
LOUISE IMOGEN GUINEY

EDITED BY
GRACE GUINEY

WITH A PREFACE BY
AGNES REPPLIER

IN TWO VOLUMES
ILLUSTRATED
VOLUME II

HARPER & BROTHERS PUBLISHERS
NEW YORK AND LONDON
MCMXXVI

 PRINTED IN THE
UNITED STATES OF AMERICA
FIRST EDITION
E-A

ILLUSTRATIONS

LETTERS OF
LOUISE IMOGEN GUINEY

LETTERS OF
LOUISE IMOGEN GUINEY

To Edmund Gosse

AUBURNDALE, MASSACHUSETTS, *June*, 1899.

MY DEAR MR. GOSSE,—It has been in my mind, for ever so long, to send you a rather nice old *Couleii Poemata*, for the Library: which capital L is written with enthusiastic respect. And now I find a chance of so doing, which seems to me as pleasant as any in the world, by the hands of a friend who is going to England, and whom, apart from that mission, I very much desire to commend to your good graces. He is Mr. Thomas Whittemore, professor of English at Tufts College, near Boston, and "a most ingeniose person" in general: I do not believe Mrs. Gosse and you have ever let over your Sunday threshold a greater lover of one John Donne, D.D., for whose *Life* we are still hungrily looking. Will you not both use him gently, for my sake? . . .

With the Cowley is a bookie for Mrs. Gosse, which I hope she may like for its novelty, though the author's name is familiarly dear to her, and not unknown to title-pages! My affectionate remembrances to her always, and to Tessa, Philip, and Sylvia the fay. I must tell you, or, rather, I will leave Mr. Whittemore to tell you, how I had the unconscionable luck to buy, the other day, a copy of H. Vaughan's *Thalia Rediviva,* 1678. It is, I think, but the fourth copy known. I have but nine seventeenth-century books: so I invite you to envy me that, and the Beaumont and Fletcher folio of 1679.

I hope Mr. Grant Richards did not fail to send you my small *England and Yesterday.* You will know where I got the golden phrase for title, but the critics either never knew, or have already forgotten: puir bodies!

Ever faithfully yours,
LOUISE IMOGEN GUINEY.

To Herbert E. Clarke

240 NEWBURY ST., BOSTON, MASS., *23rd June,* 1899.

DEAR HERBERT,—I was turrible glad to hear from you, for I've been undergoing dulness and inertia and chores, this long while, and have hardly looked a friend in the eye, by way of cordial. Then, too, I lately lost a very dear old friend, who was also a colleague of mine at the Library: Philip Savage. Did you ever run across either of his two slender books? He had a greater intimacy with the open-air world than any one I ever knew: a genuine poetic temperament, shy, gentle, brave, positive. His verse was just a bit quaintly scholastic, for all that. It reminded me sometimes of the seventeenth century lyrists, though he was Wordworth's son. Well, he died suddenly, went out in three days, quick as a candle, from the full of his life and energy. He was one-and-thirty, the best-beloved of his father's children, and engaged to the loveliest of girls: an exquisite little creature, grey-eyed and gold-haired, who breaks my heart with her tearless courage. There are a good many circumstances which made this dying especially hard to bear.—A cheerful exordium.

I rejoice that Evans tried his camera on you, and I hope you'll sit it out, "if," in the words of the immortal Grant, "it takes all summer." Your only hope is in such gentry: if indeed there can possibly be a plurality of Evanses. My duty to him. Get him to show you his photies of Ely minster; I am told they are miraculous fine. Indeed, L. C. M. is far from the vanities of London town, and peacefully anchored, arrayed in ever-modifying black, at 28 Rutland Square, Boston, U. S. A. She looks well, and has a volume of pomes going to press. I shall see her oftener now, for I also am urban. My Aunt Elizabeth and I have a great town house all to ourselves, within a stone's throw of the Public Library. The house belongs to a schoolmate of mine [1] (in the Palæozoic Age), who is at the seashore with her husband and infantry; and here we stay until September. Meanwhile, Mother farms at Auburndale, and gets visited very often, especially while cherries hang luscious on the tree!

Your translations are fine; "Orages" pleases me mightily. Cynic, but neat. I send along the one solitary rhyme the gods have suffered me to make in just eleven months.[2] It's a nasty whimper, where it isn't a catalogue, but I suppose I shall have the *ilia dura*

---

[1] Mrs. William Gregory Macdonald, *née* Katherine Kinney.
[2] "An Outdoor Litany."

ferro to put it in the book. Bliss Carman gets on, in his big unhasting way, and so does Alice Brown, who has been ill and rusticating. She has been winning much praise for a second Meadow Grass book, called *Tiverton Tales.* Poor old R. Cram has been making a DONK of himself, since he became "Prior of the No. American Cycle of the Order of the White Rose." My kind of Jacobinism is scandalized at his kind of Jacobinism.

Your mention of Victor Plarr reminded me at once of a dear little duck of a poem which I know to be his, and have by heart. I don't know one other item about him, but think he is a friend of L. Johnson's and Belgian or something: not English-born. Here's the poem.

> "A song of shadows. Never glory was
> But it had some soft shadow, that would be
> On wall, on quiet water, on smooth grass,
> Or in the vistas of the phantasy:
>
> The shadow of the house upon the lawn,
> Upon the house the shadow of the tree;
> And through the moon-steeped hours unto the dawn,
> The shadow of thy beauty over me."

I like that, don't you? It's musical and remote, and has no sense at all, and does nobody any good, bless it. Funny about the stamps. I sent the children a few better ones (old U. S. mortgage, etc., stamps) in a paper addressed to Agnes, which I hope she got. My love to her. I wish I might see her, in those unforgettable small slippers, doing every stile in Kent by the light of that best-conditioned moon. Will them ole times ever come again? Bertie must be about thirteen by now: "an old man, sir, and will be talking"!

I've been reading Aubrey's *Brief Lives* at last. As good as it can be, of the sort, and Aubrey as lovable as ever. It is just a bit over-edited by Andrew Clark, M.A., L.L.D., etc. There is in Vol. I, the most fascinating reproduction of J. A.'s Bodleian portrait. I think I must e'en have it. Which reminds me to tell you of an amazing bit of luck. You know I never buy books, never having the wherewithal. But I saw an *Olor Iscanus*, 1st edition, t'other day, and pawned my shoes and spectacles for it. The man asked a guinea, so he did; but 1651 Vaughans don't grow on every bush, do they? Well, after getting it safety home, what was my thrill to find, bound up with it, (both in nearly perfect condition) the much rarer *Thalia Rediviva*, 1678? This is the fourth copy known! The [British Museum] copy was supposed to be unique until a couple of years ago, when Miss Morgan unearthed two others, one in London, (Mr. Locker-Lampson's), one in Brecon.[1] Picture me as "perked up with majestick Pride."

Goodnight. *Vale valde.* You would not have a "seedy" minute, if I were a Christian Scientist, and Christian Science were not a sham. Did you ever try gorging with fruit? It has a distinctly jocund effect:

[1] L. I. G. presented her copy to the Bodleian Library, Oxford, in October, 1902, as "a small tercentenary gift" from "a grateful undergraduate of Sir Thomas Bodley's eternal college."

honest Injun, it has. Remember me, please, to Mr. and Mrs. Home, and tell my nephews I love 'em yet.

Yours ever,

L. I. G.

To Dora Sigerson

Autumn, 1899.

My very dear old Dora,—If it were not for one Mr. Shorter's kindness, I should not have winged you, in this fashion! I hope you have had, and are having, the very happiest of holiday tours. My own summer wound up with domestic tempests: for we have transferred ourselves from a fifteen-years' experience of what Mr. William Watson's Muse calls "rural exile," back to the heart of Boston. I am not sorry! Now when you come to America, remember that your wigwam is at 16 Pinckney St. What about your bookie? C. K. S. says something of sending me a copy of the London edition: which would delight my heart. But I have waited quite in vain to hear aught of the other from Mr. MacArthur; and now I see that he has left *The Bookman* altogether. I should be more than willing, bad reviewer as I am, to review it anywhere that I may; and I should not be afraid, I think, to try, as I really was afraid to try your father's wonderful *Gael and Gall!* For you know I have no shadow of a head, any more, and cannot put two sentences together, in prose, even. I envy the lucky souls who can grind away at the sort of labor which seems the duty of the hour *and* keep their hold on the abstract world. I know

I can't. However, it is not tragic in the least, and I do not mean to complain. Besides, I like my daily chore, which is on the Catalogue of our great Boston Public Library. Your admired Alice Brown lives nearly opposite me, and saw yesterday, for the first time, your fine big photograph of 1897. She has been in poor health for a year or more, but is improving at last. We both look back to that dear open-air summer in the blessed English valleys as our last oasis. I tell her she is "in" with the gods, whatever betide, for she can still write! You will smile when I tell you that I have a book on the very point of publication: verses, too. But they date from 1894-96. I shall ask you to put a copy on your shelf, very soon, and mark it "The dregs and lees of a poeticule." It isn't as good as your *Harp,* though I am aware the latter sets up no great standard of what's what.

I would e'en give fippence to see thee. Art a good Dreyfusard? for that is not a dead issue, by any means. Our Admiral Dewey has been here, and the whole town stood on its head, and went magnificently mad. I fear it was less for the very perfect sailor-man, than for joy at the whole Imperial-America business, which seems to me the wickedest thing I know. Some day, when I am free (*i. e.* moth-eaten and tame with years) I am going to emigrate to some hamlet that smells strong of the Middle Ages, and put cotton-wool in my ears, and swing out clear from this very smart century altogether. Now that I think of it, it must be Chilcomb, or Iffley, or Barley in Hertfordshire: so that I may get sight of Doras once in a time! Nothing like the hermit madness with method: which some of the ungodly say was Thoreau's kind. How is Hester getting on? Will you please give her my loving remembrances? I shall be writing to my dear Doctor before long. I have lost track of the gens Hinksonorum, and believe one Lionel Johnson hath become a Trappist. I hear sometimes from Mr. Gosse, . . . [End of letter missing].

To Coletta Ryan

16 PINCKNEY STREET, BOSTON, *12 Nov.*, 1899.

MY DEAR LETA,—You are a capital remodeller, and that is a rare excellence, is it not? Certainly in breadth and coherence and comprehensiveness the first version could not hold a candle to this. And yet, and yet the lyrics are still the better part. The blank verse,—may I say it?—has no beauty of its own which bears it along. It is merely a verbal bridge from song to song: your talent lies plainly in these. The spirit of the whole is noble and spiritual; ethically it is quite ideal. But we want technical skill and perfection too. You know and I know that there is nothing between the poles so difficult to achieve as the balance and rhythm of blank verse; so if we fail there, it is where a dozen very famous poets have failed before us. A great company to be damned in.

My dear, you must not be a bit disappointed that X and Company failed to accept the manuscript. I suppose the dramatic form alarmed them for one thing. Try them again with a collection of your best lyrics:

a collection which would fill eighty or one hundred pages. Don't be in haste about this, Leta. I began on that line when I was just your age, and it was much too early. So I think now, and would fain bury my first three books in the sea. Just work your golden gift as faithfully as you can, in Heaven's eye; be merciless with it until it shines forth as your best and utmost; but hold back *the Book* until you are sure by your own greater calm and simplicity and your own conscious preference of them that your poetic apprenticeship is over.

This is a hard saying; but you can stand it. Conciseness and absolute clearness are in you if you will but give them play, for they break out bright as a star on almost every page. Have you possibly loved Mrs. Browning too well? She is the worst model on earth, although a winged poet. Not that I find a single evidence of any reflected mannerism of hers in you; but your transcendentalism in particular, your rather too frequent use of the word "God," are like her to the life. If you have loved E. B. B., I think much reading of Matthew Arnold would be the best of modern antidotes.

Has the "I am" song which Francesca sings ever been printed before anywhere? I cannot remember having seen it before, and think it very beautiful. If it has not been printed, why not send it around to the *Atlantic* first, then *Harper's*, then the *Century?* Take heart, lay in a large stock of patience and purpose (*ad majoram Dei gloriam*) and go ahead, little big Leta. I believe in you for one. It has occurred to me that you may rightly have the laugh on me *à propos* of blank verse if you should see my new book: for it starts off with pages and pages of it. Only the story is the best story that ever was. So that it was impossible for me to get away from it, or treat it otherwise. I took it from the Latin almost word for word. It really isn't my affair at all, you see. Will you let me in if I come over some windy Sunday, after all these blows below the belt? We will talk of the war and the weather, and not the Muse, *nichts?*

I thank you very much for letting me see your first Symphony, Opus 1. I am sending it back after more than one reading. It has been a hard driven week for me, or I should have done it before. Write on, be happy, and reign.

My love to you,
L. I. G.

To Herbert E. Clarke

16 PINCKNEY ST., BOSTON, MASS., *13th December,* 1899.

DEAR HERBERT,—Haven't you some use for book-marks with nice Cynic or Stoic mottoes on 'em? If so, slip 'em in as you lay your book down, and a Merry Christmas to you! As I wrote Agnes the other day, we expected a call from Mrs. Strong;[1] on *her* motion, too. Well, I have nothing to report on that score, as she failed to receive my letter, and passed through Boston without seeing us. I am told by some Californian friends who know her well that she is "a fine

[1] Stevenson's stepdaughter, now Salisbury Field.

natural thing." I suppose she would have talked much of R. L. S., and I am not sure I want that. The *Letters* I haven't yet seen, but shall relish them hugely, I know, when I do. *Have* you a bicycle? What a fall (?) was there! We are having yet the most enchanting weather, but I grub indoors always, Sundays and holidays included. Mr. Collins the ex-consul, your whilom neighbor, has just been defeated as a candidate for Mayor of this town. The voting came off yesterday. He is really too nice for that business, so I'm not sorry. All the wire-pullers, "bosses," and municipal greedy Johnnies were against him. You needn't think I have too much of a *tendre* for Kruger. I can't see but that the Boers were quite right in waging war, after failing to get their reasonable way in the matter; but all the same, the British are bound to beat, and British ascendancy in So. Africa is bound to be a good thing for the world. (Why is it one always says "British" in speaking of crass public affairs, and never "English"? But "British" poetry was never heard of.)

A friend of mine, a fresh apple of a girl, who knows a lot about the seventeenth century, and is herself a painter, gave me lately a jolly little portrait in copper of K. Charles II, which she picked up in a sort of junk-shop in Bath, last summer. It is certainly contemporaneous with the Puritan maiden just-named (I don't mean Harriet Barnes, as you will have discovered!) and I dare say it was painted from life. About 1655 seems to be the date, during the exile at Brussels or Breda. We mean to identify it more fully sometime. A curio of that sort is very rare, and it constitutes at present the chief joy of my life. It is oval in shape, and as big as a big locket would be. The colors are clear, but the copper is flaky with age.

The boys' Aunt Lou is a hollow fraud this year, but I hope they will write to her, to comfort her "feelinks," and tell her what their Christmas haul was. Wish every one of them a stockingful for me. I forgot to say I was mighty pleased that Sydney liked "Tyrone." It is, at any rate, as good now as I can make it; and it was your own sage advice which set me to bettering it, else I should have thrown it away in despair.

Yours affectionately,

L. I. G.

To Dora Sigerson

16 Pinckney St., Boston, Mass., *18th March,* 1900.

My dearest Dora,—It is long since your gifts came, and so the thanks kept on accumulating. The books are among my treasures. You have gone forward gloriously; and I am sinfully proud of the likes of you! Among so many old numbers which I have long loved, so many new ones which one comes on with a fresh shock of delight in their free grace and sincerity, I must tell you that the two which took hold of me so that I had to go up and down stairs repeating them, were two which, in the London edition, come together: "False Dearbhorgill," and "Ireland." Such a ballad! and such a lyric! They sting: as beauty can always do.

How are you, colleen? My Mother, like almost all our fellow-beings over here, had a tussle this winter with the Influenza, but is up and about again, as straight and pink-cheeked as ever. I am well, busy, and deadly dull, always dreaming of going back to England, and editing my beloveds of the seventeenth century. I am afraid that is the only Paradise I hunger for, now that I live in a world underground, where no fine arts nor belles-lettres grow, and where one's chief business is

> "——to come it brave and meek
> On thirty bob a week!"

However, I happened to see the first two numbers of a periodical called *The Sphere,* in whose manner and appearance I was hugely interested. You would have sworn, from its calm and knowing air, that it had been seated in the Strand since the Norman Conquest. Shall you visit Ireland, this spring? If you do, I charge you to tell your father and Hester that I think of them very, very often, and with never-ceasing affection. When there swings into the starry line another Piatt poet, I am in hopes to see Hester in this native hemisphere of mine. It can't compare with the other for quiet, and twilight, and ivied memories, and a soil of dreams. But there are "sky-scraper" buildings, and canvas-back ducks. I sometimes have wondered why Mr. Shorter has never come back with you, O bonnie shallop! in tow. There would be welcomes, as he must know well.

An old friend of mine, an ex-publisher, a great bibliophile, and a most distinguished amateur in photography and kindred arts, F. Holland Day, is going to London in April, for a year or so. He wishes to know you and

Mr. Shorter; so I will send him along, unless you curse me meanwhile, and cry "Forbear!" My book reached you, did it not? and my letter, posted to your Paris address last October? We continue to enjoy town life again. By that, I do not mean gayeties, etc., for I never have time to go about any more. How are your pets? Is your parrot as pretty as this, which a talkative friend of mine shed the other day? Miss Morgan and I are about to edit a Vaughan together (*Silex Scintillans* only), for the Temple Classics: unless Mr. Gollancz takes alarm at having called up *two* female spectres. He addressed Miss Morgan as "Dear Sir." Isn't she a Fine Thing? She "took" mightily to you. A man in Oxford, Mr. W. H. Hadow, whom I never saw, but whose books I know, has set my Irish Peasant Song No. 1 to the most exquisite plaintive music in E. I wish you might hear it sometime. It is in a volume with others: Arthur Symons and myself in company with the high gods: Blake, Scott, Stevenson, and a'. Goodnight, dear Dora. Let me hear from you ever and anon, for old times' sake. Commend me to C. K. S., and believe me Ever yours,

LOUISE I. GUINEY.

To Herbert E. Clarke

16 PINCKNEY ST., BOSTON, *9th May,* 1900.

DEAR HERBERT,—Better were it not to think your thoughts of me! I am a castaway and a shirk: that's flat. It's Influenza and its train; also and chiefly, it is cussed low spirits, the long green-sickness, I take it, of imminent middle age, for I haven't *lived* in the Pit since I was seventeen or so. And really, the only decent thing is to get into a hole, and stay there, and hang sociabilities! until one is fit for the eye of friends. I'm under a deadly homesickness for Liberty and Litteryture,—yea, and for Fleet St., E. C. I forge along for weeks and months, aye cataloguing for all I am worth; but that's the chronic situation. *You* would scarce suspect, however dumb I remained, that I was looking for Some One to Love me; but I thought it could not fail to please you, on La Rochefoucauld's principle, to know the true cause of the eclipse of an optimist. No, Sir, I have no sort of pot-boiler in mind, whereby I shall continue to live in Lunnon after I get there, presumably in the character of stowaway; but I'll quote you one Montrose about fearing one's fate too much. Wait until next year! for explode I must not until then. Perhaps I can peddle water-cresses. The pastoral appeals to my taste.

Your shamrock was fair to see, and most welcome. I hope you may dance soon again over the relief of Mafeking. I get Britisher and Britisher, as time passes, possibly because my native land is Boerizing. Thank you for the Lecky article; I was heartily converted long ere that, and drink daily to the confusion of Kruger and his—Roundheads. By F. H. Day, who must even now be meandering in the classic purlieus of Bloomsbury, I sent you a small work which I hope you will find irreverently pleasing. Oh, say! I have you, concerning the "misprint" of "boy" for "dog" on p. 57, of my little *Arnold.* If you were a doggy character, which you are not (and I consider that, sir, your chief moral shortcoming), you would know by instinct that what Arnold, who *was* a doggy character, wrote, was just "boy," and naught else. Every doggy character uses "boy" and "man" in the vocabulary of endearment applied to a deserving canine! But what know you of these transcendental matters, O literalist? As for my preface, what's the use of saying stuff you discover, or remember, has been well said already? Hence Galton: though it is killingly in Arnold's own donnish prose manner. But it is the identical thing I wanted to emphasize and wind up with. Would to Heaven I could not read, but only write! for then I should be, who knows? a rale janius. (Observe that no remark of this complexion can be properly called conceit, emanating, as it does, from one long retired into private life.)

The *Silex Scintillans* fell through, temporarily, anyhow, if not for good. It seems that in Mr. Gollancz's absence, through illness, Dent's printers got unmanageable, and set up in cast pages, a bad old text of Pickering's Vaughan, 1858, which was intended for galley, and for me to use as basis of the revise. The business is so expensive, that, errors and all, Dent feels he must issue it. He wishes Miss Morgan and me to use our MSS. on a second edition of his *Silex,* as neither of us would now have anything to do with this hybrid publication. Also, we are asked to look after the secular poems; I suppose we shall do so, though there is but a beggarly fee. I have been much interested in Mr. [Bertram] Dobell's articles, so well-thought-out and well-expressed, in the *Athenæum,* concerning the MS. poems which Dr. Grosart was ready to swear were H. V.'s. He copied some of them to show me, as soon as he had examined them; and unlike any other interested critic whose opinion he sought, I held out against that supposed authorship with all my might. So that now one Traherne looms on the horizon, I feel the virtuous glow of whoso should say "I told 'ee so." The poems are the real thing, don't you think? and stand yet more alone by their fine philosophy than by their quaint music. There were Trahernes in Glamorganshire, in the Silurist's own time, and distantly related to him, I think. I have left no space to tuck in my messages to Agnes and the four. But I love 'em, and don't care who knows it. You, too, when you're good! As ever,

L. I. G.

To Gelett Burgess

16 PINCKNEY ST., BOSTON, *27th May*, 1900.

MY DEAR LUPE,[1]—You may guess whether I thank you! But I did not know you were a Friar Minor, a San Franciscan in that sense: and since you are, the joke is on you for giving me anything so precious. My own passion, all my life, has been non-collecting. I too would "fly light and be ready to wing when I'm called." I never have the heart to keep a gift long; the few rare books and curios I have are all affianced to others: even R. L. S.'s lock of hair, in the little silver case, I mean to leave in the Bodleian before I die.[2] But I shall be

[1] Lupe, Samoan for "lark," was a name given by Mrs. Stevenson to Gelett Burgess when he was editor of *The Lark*. It is a dissyllable.

[2] This lock of hair, in its case, was given to the Bodleian Library 5 June, 1906. L. I. G. also gave that Library, 21 July, 1904, a ring containing a lock of Keats's hair.

a mother to that bookie, and your profound debtor evermore. I can't help loving you better, moreover, for being a monk of my own Order, as aforesaid. Perish the gathererin! "I have little," says old Burton, "I want nothing: all my treasure is in Minerva's tower."

The news of the poems is most welcome. You won't find a more gallant title than *A Gage of Youth*. Say: wouldn't you like my old *Patrins* better than verses? . . . (I'm done up, you know: no more literary rockets and pin-wheels. It rains and rains. So you won't mind an 1897 book.) Goodnight, and *bonne aventure!* Salute one Bruce Porter for me.

Yours,
L. I. GUINEY.

To Gelett Burgess

16 PINCKNEY STREET, BOSTON, *Memorial Day*, 1900.

DEAR LUPE,—The Friars Minor, you know, are just Franciscans, the society founded by St. Francis of Assisi: his cardinal principle in life was not to own things, *i.e.*, not to let 'em own you, and he stood up to it literally, and while his followers were true to him they were happy as "a threadbare goldless genealogie." Then they began to have houses, and pocketbooks, and two coats, and the darling Order went to smash for a long time. Socrates was by nature a Franciscan; so was Thoreau; but not all philosophers are so in love with the nude! Somewhere in *Patrins* the undersigned must have held forth on this very choice topic; perhaps in "The Precept of Peace": only I am too lazy to look. . . .

I shall send the book to you in California, sometime between now and Michaelmas. Good luck overtake you, or lie in wait and pounce upon you: Amen. It is eminently proper that you lit upon my name. They used to call me at school (from mine exceeding mildness and tractableness) Le Loup-Garou.

Yours meanwhile,

L. I. G.

To Herbert E. Clarke

10 YARMOUTH ST., BOSTON, *13th Nov.*, 1900.

MY DEAR LONG-ENDURING MAN,—Funny things have happened since I addressed this envelope on Sunday. First, I sallied forth, and sprained my ankle: "a thing," as the comic song says, "which we've never done before," and I was promptly laid up in elegant leisure at home, fairly delighted that at last I am sure to answer that letter, and a score of others less desirable. (Let me add that I am getting on famously, and am lying shod in a surgical rubber thong, and shall surely be back at my library work in a very few days now.) Then yesterday L. C. M. sent me word that she was in town: and to-day comes a second message, saying that she has brought me books for a gift from you. Lo, this covereth me with confusion as with a garment! The only book I deserve would be *The Curse of Kehama*. But before I post this I shall be able to thank you specifically for the articles, as I do now, most heartily, for the deed.

I amused myself last night with scoring off, in Dobell's November catalogue, a few £5 items which I should be well-pleased to buy. He seems to get hold of a good number of first-edition Hazlitts. I think his show of seventeenth-century stuff is always more than fair. To speak true, I've been depleting, not increasing, our small library, since we let the Pinckney St. house in September. (You know my Mother was in Maine all summer long, and my Aunt and I luxuriating alone at that spacious 240 Newbury St.) I gave almost all my Father's books to his old College,[1] and sold a couple of hundred for which I had no mortal use. If you had been near, I fancy we might have made some pleasing exchanges. I mean to go on de-collecting: it is entirely in my line.

Well, having quitted our "tent of a night" at Pinckney St. (a dear quaint neighbourhood) we took to boarding for a while; and here I am, two decks up in the air, aft, over some big yards with poplars and grape-vines, very near L. C. M., very near the big Library. And "here shall I die ashore" not quite: because I am going to sail for England by the end of January, or the first of the following month. I am taking with me my sole Aunt, who has had no end of hard luck with her eyes, and who will profit greatly by escaping most of the winter glare upon our New England snow. We mean to put into the port of Plymouth, and stay in Devon for a couple of months. Next, I want to see Miss Morgan in Brecon, a Petticoats whom I already love dear, without seeing; and I rather think, once I get to Wales, that I shall try to cross over to Ireland. (It is all a question of shillings and shoe-

[1] Holy Cross, Worcester, Mass.

leather.) Anyhow, I shall strike London in July, *"Deo volente et diabolo nolente."* And the very first thing I shall do there, after hugging all the 'bus-horses and all the Bobbies, will be to fly down to see you and Agnes and my nevvies dear. Perhaps you'll take me to see Evans and the Hinksons, who have returned to Ealing. (I've forgotten my way west, but not south.) Some bird or other,—it was George Barton, to name the very duck,—told me that there is a Mrs. Evans. This strikes one's sense of the supernatural. I hope her lord is as happy as he surely deserves to be, and by way of making more of his exquisite pictures. I like yours better and better, though I liked it greatly from the first. It is one of the few on my [landlady's] wall here.

We had a caller since we came here: Mrs. Strong, Stevenson's step-daughter. (This is his fiftieth birthday, is it not?) She is a natural, kindly, talkative woman, very short and rather wide, with big black eyes; might be a Samoan native. Not the remotest literary sense that I could scent. I am told on all sides that she never had her mother's charm. Capable, one is pretty sure, and good to live with, and affectionate. She didn't take greatly to me, I suspect. She goes about lecturing (on R. L. S., etc.) and is successful at it. I could show you a privately-printed booklet she gave me, containing poems chiefly addressed to Tuila,[1] herself. Perfectly futile verses they be. The dear R. L. S. has been hard-driven.

Nov. 14. Well. *don't* I thank you, H. E. C.! I

[1] Samoan name meaning "the adorner," given to Mrs. Strong.

feel like the day after Christmas, what with all these fine presents and testimonials. Last evening *meine Mutter* went over to interview L. C. M., and returned with an armful to rejoice my heart. You are a regular old prince, anyhow, aren't you? The Dobell[1] is a treasure; I always liked the old rawhead and bloody bones, a straggler from the rear guard of "the spacious times," but never owned a copy of my own. And the defence of The Blessed Martyr, Limited, is a nice thing, and new to me. It had the dearest little old portrait print of "Carolus Agnus" on the fly-leaf, pasted in: did you put it there, or did it grow? I find that I agree with your enthusiastic scoring of "The Night": it's orful stuff, smelling rank of Maeterlinck, all along the line. Not that I don't admire Maeterlinck, at least aside from his dramas, vastly; but an alien odour is never exactly a fragrance, no matter from whom or from what it proceedeth. Then there's Tutin's shapely edition of poor Smart.[2] I read the "David" over at once; and I must tell you that the one phrase which I found absolutely fresh in my memory is: "the quick peculiar quince." This is superfine, and equal to the raptures. Isn't it by those light homely touches, so bitingly true, for all their rhetoric, that we detect poets? The whole fun of reading is in such suggestions, or discoveries. Has there been any poet since "A Shropshire Lad"? I love that acrid mournful little book. Certainly, we have no new one here. Mr. Stedman's too fat American Anthology is out. He will

[1] Sydney Thompson Dobell (1824–1874), poet and critic.
[2] Christopher Smart (1722–1771), poet.

have made L. C. M. cross, I fear, by calling her "Ellen Louise (Chandler) Moulton": a rather stupid specification, at this hour o' day. My Mother thinks she looks tired, and is losing zest, for which I am sorry; but I shall surely see her next week, and provoke her all I can, with intent to cheer and not inebriate. . . .

A. Brown is in great form these days, and is like to make a fortune yet: a game which plays ducks and drakes with me. I am going to claim alimony the moment she waxes rich. My love, at a steady 100 per cent, to Agnes, also to her young eagles. I thought of a once very small Francis, the other day, when I heard a proud Mamma boasting of the "mar-vellous memory" of her twenty-year-older, who had learned by rote, the "Ancient Mariner" in *two days*. (He is, by the way, and always has been, one of the stupidest and most worthless of boys.) I wish you would tell me, "private-like," whether any of the children have watches of their own? I have recently bestowed on myself a darling Yankee invention, sufficiently light, and truthful to a degree, costing 87 cents; and I made up my mind at once that Santa Claus really ought to know in good season whether time has already established personal relations with those four young gentlemen? If not, why not? Wouldn't it add punctuality to their virtues, and vanity to their vices, bless 'em? No man can say the price is loud, although the tick-tick-tick is. Goodnight.

Yours ever affectionately,

L. I. G.

To Herbert E. Clarke

BOSTON, *13th Dec.*, 1900.

MY DEAR HERBERT,—"Sandy Clause, who is a miff, but suts a bootiful miff!" is posting you one proud, and one humble parcel. The former has the American Anthology (a poor comrade, so far as the essentials go, for your mateless Victorian of the two-shilling barrow, but still its mate); and the other has some trifles for the children. No end of luck and cheer and love to you all for Christmas!

I may not write again until I do so under a Devon post-mark, along in Feb., 1901. My ankle is rather thick yet, but all right for walking, and disposed to prance through Hayes, Addington, and Shirley. I'll race you, too, despite some 22 grey hairs! all in a clump. . . .

You say naught, this long while, of Mr. Home. I do hope he is well. I've been reading the State Trials of Charles II's time, in the contemporary folio reports, lately: Stafford's, Russell's, and the whole Titus Oates business: the most amazing web of lies, full of interstices and bits of daylight to *us*. Wonderful and abominable that it was ever believed a whole piece of cloth, and cloth of gold at that! You see I haven't your courage strange countries for to see, in the way of Spanish classics; when my blood is up, I take the trolley-car to the seventeenth century.

Oh! I knew you'd fly at me for my screed on V. R. I. The fact is, I wrote it before I had heard of the nawsty French disrespect, etc., otherwise, as a bit of private taste, I should have suppressed it. Not that *that* lady can ever mean England to me. But it is mean to plague her; and I would fain punch in person the misguided Gaul who can't see his perfide Albion in the abstract. My own animad-versions (privately printed) are, as you will have perceived, based on poetics, and not on politics. Come! for the sake of Agnes's Irish great-grandmother, shake hands on it. It is freezing here. My breath to Heaven like vapor goes; may my soul follow at an indefinitely prorogued period. *Auf wiedersehen, liebeswürdiger Mann.*

L. I. G.

To the Rev. W. H. van Allen

10 YARMOUTH ST., BOSTON, *30th December*, 1900.

MY DEAR FRIEND,—Haven't you been good to me, and ben't I a Pig? I have sat, as Sir Thomas Browne says, "in the soft showers of Providence." No! it was Bishop Jeremy Taylor who said it: but my wits stumble, these days, what with B. P. L., and ships at sea, and books and papers to pack, and Conscience pulling me ever by the sleeve, and reminding me of my own shameful shortcomings, under the Yuletide star. Late as it is, I beg leave to wish you blessings and things! And I thank you a thousand warm times for the dear bookie of fine verses, and the beautiful S. Monica, whose son is my very particular patron and ideal. She makes me wish I were bound for Five Islands instead of Devon, so that I might get her framed, and enshrined upon a wall of our very own. I don't know even yet just when

I sail, for the lists for January are delayed: but it is somewhere about the 22nd, from New York. Be sure to let me do you any useful turn over there that I can: bookish or otherwise . . .

Mother sends her New Year's greeting with mine. *Accendat in nobis Dominus ignem sui amoris et flammam æternae caritatis!* That is the only wish worth while; and you will know the source whence I have it in my ears.[1] I thank you, too, for the Royal Standard, and your all too handsome bay-leaf tossed to a played-out, toil-eaten poeticule, who is ever

Yours faithfully,
L. I. G.

To Mrs. E. D. Jordan

DARTMOUTH, DEVON, *21 March,* 1901.

DEAR LITTLE MOTHER JORDAN,—I am a Bad Lot never to have thanked you and the Family for that beautiful box which greeted us aboard the *Devonian*. To say it was appreciated hardly expresses how touching it was to have you remember your wayfarer with gifts, at such a time. If I had not loved you all along, how I could fall in love with you now! I must be frank, and own that most of the delicious contents accompanied us ashore. Aunty was complimented by the Captain (a fine bluff Scotchman, Muir by name) and the Doctor (a handsome and sweet-mannered Irishman) as a perfect seawoman: but of course I lay in misery and disgrace for eight of our ten warm, sunny, smooth Atlantic days.

[1] The Mass.

I did make out to attack the grape-fruit, though, and to hold to it, in a menu-less world. It is a capital ship, and highly recommendable to Jordans, for future possible emergencies. Never were better staterooms, or a daintier table (*non* experto crede!) or a more unsmelling and unrolling whole. I spent a good part of my short time on deck among the splendid doomed bullocks below; we carried some seven hundred head of them, and most comfortably accommodated they were. One big fellow was as much given to chin-kissing as ever Lillo was. There were about a dozen high-bred horses, also extremely cordial; one of these died, poor fellow, of what one of the attendant sailors laconically described to me as "gripes"; and him we buried at sea, off the Irish coast. There were but three other passengers. Aunty's foot went back on her as soon as we reached London; so for some days I had everything to do. She is all right now, and professes to like England: which contents me hugely. I am dreadfully dull as yet, and cannot use my head at all. This is a crazily, dingily picturesque little town which you would love, because it is so full of

> "murmurs and scents of the infinite sea!"

The site is exactly similar to our Five Island cottages: I mean we look directly across the Dart, at a rocky house-dotted shore, and indirectly out to the open sea. The walk to the castle harbor-mouth is inexpressibly romantic, and out there, at either side, the surf is pounding tremendously just now in the equinoctial wind. The girls would find some excitement, as I do, in looking at that surf where the sun strikes it; for what colour should you guess it to be? White-crested, of course, but otherwise a rich dazzling, startling blood-red! The sandstone soil does the business; all the new ploughed fields in Devon are the same glorious tint. Take a silver-olive sort of a sea, with crimson breakers all along a craggy strand, against the vividly green springtime landscape, and we have pictures for Tom Meteyard, or anybody of that persuasion.

Dartmouth itself is great fun. It hangs on a steep hillside, tier above tier of venerable gabled houses crowding one another; and every cross-street is a long stone staircase, full of lichens and copperish weather-stains, fumbling a way up into the sky, with curious windings, and little low walls overhung with ivy and fern and snap-dragon. We lodge in a tiny square where we have two cosy rooms, and most capital kindly attendance and good cooking, all for 10s. a week; and from our own ancient windows I cannot see a single roof or doorstep which can possibly date from later than James I.'s time. This is invigorating to a belated mediævalist, isn't it? My questionable friend Charles II. was here once, and as it is raining, I am going around this afternoon to see the interior of a much-carved and chimney-pieced, timbered and colonnaded house which sheltered the royal head. We hear the curfew and the town-crier; we eat clotted cream; we smell tides and fishing nets all day long. The whole place is another Marblehead, only of stone, and queerer. As Aunty enjoys it as much as I do, we shall stay on for some eleven days more, and then go up-river to Totnes. Please tell Alice that I have discovered, to my joy, that Herrick's Dean Prior lies within seventeen miles, and of course he is buried there; hence it follows that I have another literary call to make, presently.

I did not succeed very definitely in London, as to "portable chores," owing to finding one publisher-man absent, and the other not greatly to my mind: a contingency which always throws me into a bad light, and makes me seem, and be, unnecessarily stupid. But neither have I cause to despair; and at any rate, I am inclined to loaf until June, so long as I can do so at last without shirking some manifest duty. Wherever we "move on," the Brown, Shipley address, is the right one. A month from now will find me, I dare say, beginning again on that beloved and troublesome bard, Henry Vaughan, among his own Breconshire primroses.

Next time I shall write Mary. I miss her, wherever there are roads and channels. My love to her, please, as to Alice. You must be a proud Mamma of a young person who at so infantile an official age, can run a whole department! There are days when I am restless enough to wish myself back at that absorbing work, where one Mistress Mackay, I hear, is in possession of my abandoned diggings. The Bodleian is announcing its three-hundredth anniversary festival for next year, with invitations to all Universities and all Libraries to follow; so perhaps I shall see New-Englanders, if I sit patiently betimes upon an Oxford stile. Aunty sends you her love. We heard from Marmee lately; she was doing bonnily at 16 Pinckney St. Goodnight, and all blessings, from

Your affectionate old
L. I. G.

To Mary Jordan

DARTMOUTH, DEVON, *31st March*, 1901.

DEAREST MARY,—Wherever there be sea-smells, I am especially sure to miss you. There's nothing to beat this queer enchanting town, caught up into a hillside, like a gull's nest in a crag, and full of

"—sailors with bearded lips,
The beauty and mystery of the ships,
And the magic of the sea."

I have discovered that our *Mayflower* lay here at anchor a whole week, with all the patriarchs aboard. It interests me a bit more, being farther back, that Richard Lionheart got all his crusaders together here in Dertemouthe, and that his long galleys put off from this same deep and smiling harbor.

Aunty has had a tremendous cold; but as soon as she began to better, I turned loose out-of-doors, on all-day walks, some of them pretty rough scrambles. And such weather for the "English Riviera!" Bitter cold; the most violent land-winds I ever faced; and on Friday, *eleven* distinct and sharp snow-storms, punctuated by a fat, innocent-looking joker of a sun, whom you longed to shoot at sight. The countryside is lovely with daffodils, and loud with larks and finches; and it's quite exciting to an American solitary to stir up, every mile or two when you are not on the high-road, a covey of pheasants, or the whole white-behinded populace of a rabbit-warren. I've seen many things I wanted to see, and some I didn't look for. One was a yew of a thousand years and more: a giant patriarch, lovingly propped up by a whole forest of poles, at Stoke Gabriel. Another was an old enchanting place, Dartington Hall, where, as I suddenly remembered, Francis Champernowne was born. I forget whether you know Gerrish Island, off Kittery, Maine, and Celia Thaxter's old home there? When I was a youngster, I used to see the lone cairn of stones, in the field next the shore, under which that good gentleman of Devon has slept since 1647. "Chauncey's Creek," which you'll find on any chart of that locality, is a corruption of "Champernowne's Creek." So the sight of the hall was like a breath of home, or a link between two ages and two worlds. But for the most part my marches have been in wilder places. We live in two sizable, comfortable rooms, the rent whereof (including everything except the actual cost of what we eat) is $2.40 (10/.) per week. I nearly bankrupted myself buying some books I wanted to work from, in London; but now we begin to fatten again, and aspire to spend Easter week in Totnes, Modbury, Torquay, and Plymouth. They're all close by; Modbury, I fancy, will be a matter of two hours or so. It is too soon yet for many American letters, and we miss the enlightening visits of the worthy *Transcript,* for which we simply must re-subscribe. Aunty has transferred her interests, I tell her, to one King Edward and his posterity; it is quite paralysing to hear how glib she has become on the subject. She is a brick, and really does seem to get enjoyment out of what I feared would be a lonely experiment for her. Did you know that Mam had moved across the road to Fred Day's cosy rooms? . . .

I am going to set my heart on the summer of 1902, for a reason. Always provided I shall be here! I accomplished nothing very definite in London, among the publisher-men, but will go back there in June with a clearer head, ready for events. Mr. Alfred Nutt, who has published a lot of books touching the "Celtic Revival," was exceedingly nice to me. Have you seen Prof. Dowden's new book, *Anglican and Puritan?* It sounds theological; but it is only a meek literary affair of much charm. Goodnight, my deary-O. Keep well, and don't forget

Yours to love you,
L. I. G.

To the Rev. W. H. van Allen

DARTMOUTH, DEVON, PASSION SUNDAY, *1st April,* 1901.

How goes it with you, Anglicanissime? You should be here to foot it in the winds of Dartmoor, all along a silver-green sea with surf of dazzling rose-red, among larks and daffodils, and clotted cream and things! We lodge in a crazy square, in a Jacobean house now grown rowdy, next an interesting ancient parish church, which has yet its glorious wooden Perpendicular chancel-screen, and on its later pulpit, something which would delight your historic sense, to wit:

C R
1646

As I haunt the place, I frequently meet Vicar or Curate coming forlornly in (during Lent, too!) to read the service to a congregation of one woman.

The town is like Marblehead, only a thousand times steeper, more unexpected, more romantic. The streets are staircases, dripping, foreign-looking, ivy-hung, full of gables and dormer-windows, and smells of the pure living water below. My Aunt has been only pretty well, so far, on land, though she made a famous record aboard ship; but she is progressing. We shan't go back to London before June; between that and us lie pleasant vistas of Oxford and of Wales. I told you once, I think, of my *tendre* for Hurrell Froude? By way of bankrupting myself, I bought in London his *Remains* (4 vols. Rivingtons, 1838-40) for £3. 17; and have been re-reading them with more than my old interest. When I can write a bit again, I shall do what I can to make the anti-theologs love him. I found his grave last week, in the rain, at Dartington: a strangely solemn little village nook, where a battered tower alone remains of the mediæval church he knew. The clear grassy space meant to me, the nave, the chancel, the altar-stone, O NOT of the belief "by law established"! I knelt down there. Saw you Gerrish Island ever? at the farther end of Kittery, Maine, nigh Portsmouth? If so, you will remember the lone cairn of a dear gentleman, Francis

Champernowne, laid there in 1647. He was born at Dartington Hall, where

> "year by year his memory fades
> From all the circle of the hills."

Indeed, this whole neighborhood spells enchantment, tradition, peace. I won't go home till morning!

Your admirer, my parent, has moved across Pinckney Street into Fred Day's rooms at No. 9, intending Five Islands by June, and a chase after her flown bird, if all goes well, in September. Despite my tranquil estate, I miss divers Bostonians besides this one; yea, I miss even the damp evening smell of the godly *Transcript*. All good to you along your way. "Ah, idle creature!" as Millamant says in the best comedy ever written. You have my standing address? (Lie it does not, owing to some infirmity.) My friend Herbert Clarke lately bought for a shilling, off a barrow in the London streets, a *Roadside Harp in red:* surely one of your brood? *Sane quidem;* or I rave.

Ever yours,
L. I. G.

To Margaret Haskell

DARTMOUTH, DEVON, *April 10th,* 1901.

DEAR OLD MARGARET,—*Wie gehts?* This is from my hill-top (urban, rainy, Jacobean) to yours. I could wish you in Dartmouth, these blossomy days, by a more vivid colored sea than any I know, and among the bright red ploughed furrows of neighboring hills, where I walk and walk, dogless and alone, to use up my fine first month of rest. The countryside is full of rain, every day, but the rain makes daffodils, and by a more circuitous process, clotted cream. You would like the funny venerable steep little town, a hundred times wilder and more romantic than our Marblehead, but reminding you of it at every turn. Did you know (I didn't) that the Pilgrim Fathers lay a week in harbor here, aboard the *Mayflower,* before setting sail for U. S. A.? I get more poetical nourishment, however, out of that other as-well-authenticated fact that Richard Lionheart got his gilded galleys together in the same waters, *anno* 1180, and streamed away processionally on his Crusade. The place has a purple-and-gold history and is crowded with ancient architectural survivals. It is all staircases, too, like pictures one sees of Amalfi. On a blowy day the surf is a riot of color, like Jacqueminot roses. A *silver*-sanded beach is rare here. . . .

Goodnight, lassie. All good to you and to you-alls, from Aunty and your ever affectionate

L. I. G.

To Miss Charlotte E. Maxwell[1]

DARTMOUTH, DEVON, *10 April,* 1901.

DEAREST MISS MAXWELL,—Here are primroses. Don't I wish for you among the hills all golden with them, under the unceasing showers! But I forget that

[1] Her gymnasium in Boston L. I. G. attended regularly for several years. Miss Eleanor Deane was Miss Maxwell's assistant.

you are not so much a muddy-booted Knight, by nature, as I am, nor so fond of "Shanks' mare!" I am loafing altogether, hearing thrushes, poking into ancient wayside Churches, sleeping, devouring clotted cream, and talking to baa-lambs through the budding hedges. It is all very fine, though it doesn't seem to make a ghost of an idea germinate in my vacant head. This Dartmouth is like another Marblehead, only with its beauty and its oddity, its age and charm, intensified a hundred fold. The countryside is even better than the town. I miss my dog, along the roads. But it is a refreshment (stupidly piggy as the remark looks, it is not so) to be alone, after long being one of a company, at one mill-wheel or another. I have found one friend at least over here in need of your Swedish evangel: my dear Harry Hinkson, who is husband of the poet Katharine Tynan. His theory is that as he cannot now keep his horse, he is perishing for lack of exercise, there being nothing else violent enough to suit his worship. If you and Miss Deane come over and start a propaganda, there's a very nice recruit for you. I hope they all go bonnily, your merry men! Rather easier to handle, don't you think, than that ridiculously-hampered class at the Convent? I have always been so deadly ashamed of those nunnies' Philistinism.

I fly to Miss Morgan on the 23rd; then Oxford, for some reading at the Bodleian; and London again. . . . Changes are abroad in London. It looks grievous to see an immense section of the Strand, on the north side, coming down; but at Westminster, one does not, somehow, miss King Street. And the new vista of the Abbey, from Whitehall, is very fine. It has been, everywhere here, a dreary March, cold and wet, full of storms. My Aunt gets on beautifully, nevertheless; and I am very well too. I suppose Marmee doesn't get over to see you, she is so full again of never-ending bother about No. 16. Our poor dear lessee has died lately. She (Marmee) is nested like a cuckoo in Fred Day's pleasant rooms at No. 9, until his return in May or June.

On boat and train, we took turns reading *The Cardinal's Snuff-box.* Isn't it a delicious little story? Tell my dear Miss Deane I love her yet, and am ever, as our Yankee idiom neatly puts it,

Hern and Yourn,
L. I. G.

To Mrs. F. H. Briggs

2 Ship Street, Oxford, *9th July,* 1901.

Dearest Ada,—I am going to send you, by F. H. D., next month, a little old picture which I carried off from a Welsh landlady. It hung on my wall in Brecon, and amused me both by being entitled "Ada" and by looking more or less like you. It will, I doubt not, remind your Mother of you as you were in 1840!

Many a time I have thought of you, and meant to write; but I was, and am, too afraid of being dismal. Aunty has been lying ill (with but one partial respite, during which I took a week's attempted, but not very successful, rest, in Wales) ever since April 15th. My only converse is with Drs. and Nurses. Everything else came long ago to a dead standstill. She cannot, poor dear, ever be well again, though now she suffers little. The hardest thing to bear is that she is very often out of her mind, and looks on all the world (including, alas, me who love her) as her enemy and persecutor. So you see I have no news. My Mother is in Maine, where she has not succeeded yet in selling our pleasant little roof-tree on the coast. I wonder where you and Fred are? I certainly do wish I might see you, these beautiful cool English days. My love to him; to ever dear "Aunt Mary," who will keep well and happy if I have any political pull on the gods; and to my old friend, the head of the family. Also to Mrs. Langley. And likewise (don't forget!) to Jock o' Sharon.

Yours affectionate
L. I. G.

To the Rev. W. H. van Allen

2 Ship Street, Oxford, *July 24,* 1901.

Reverende: (*Hoc licet tibi!*)—Your seemly script gives me a pang; for I had sworn to myself and to the Honble Mrs.[1] to write you, weeks ago. I couldn't budge from Oxford, my Aunt having been so dreadfully ill again; but she came up to see me, from London, and we played together a whole evening, cursed the modern world, and exchanged ideas about you, over what *she* considered a very bad dinner, at the Clarendon. Then we had an hour together next morning in the Physick Garden, opposite Magdalen tower, before she sped to Ireland. She is a Fine Thing: tall, not thin; young; full

[1] The Hon. Ermengarda Greville-Nugent.

of humour and perception; Continental rather than English, Scots, or Irish; a good talker; holding vehement and fixed opinions; and with an air of charm and wilfulness which I find not uncommon to only children. Altogether, she reminded me in personal traits, as she had already done on paper, of—you. You would be called wondrous alike, were you brother and sister. Your inconsequent, cocksure, and all-appropriating Anglicanism is exactly the same in either.

Not a scrap of news can I give; I have lived indoors since April set in, with Nurses and my poor invalid. To-day she sat up, for the first time, and I hope to be able to take her very shortly into the hillier country, close by; but both Drs. say she never can be her robust self again. As for plans, "one step enough for me." I am violently interested in my Mother's forthcoming decision, whether to come over or no. Not a stroke of my own dear work have I been able, so far, to do.

Clement Shorter sent me to-day a royal gift: the Goupil Charles II. When I can sit down to read it, I know not. Why do you not come over to Oxford, where your battered friend S. Bernard looks down on S. Giles Street from his outer niche in S. John's College? How could you better spend a holiday? One month, forty pounds: and 'tis done. I have always wished, for my part, to live and die here. I tell Aunty we are on ancestral ground! for that bold Norman Robert d'Oyley built the big tower next door but one, by whose ancient and not unmelodious four-bell chime we keep the hours. My best thanks for the *Messages* and the copy of your philippic on the Scriptures. Whenever you go East, and see Lees, tell them I love them yet, and gaze daily upon all their effigies, aligned upon my writerless desk. It has been hot even here, and

"the big rain came dancing to the earth"

this afternoon. Goodnight, my acquitted Bishop. What a humming diocese yours would be! But "wait till you come to forty year," or else rival John XXII, (wasn't it?) who was Pope while in bib and tucker. Before I close, I must tell you that the Vicar of this parish called to offer Aunty his ministrations, and took exquisitely my disclaimer. He is a son of Dr. Merry, Warden of Lincoln College.

Ever yours, though but "seedy,"
L. I. G.

To Dora Sigerson

2 Ship St., Oxford, *Aug. 5th,* [1901.]

Dearest Dora,—Being rather homesick for sight or sound of you, I decided to write you, and let the Editor-man pick up what belongs to him out of his wifey's correspondence. I am so glad you are in that nice fat calm Buckinghamshire, full of roses and pheasants and things: "an abominably tidy landscape," my friend Bruce Porter once called it; and I do hope it is doing you a world of good, dear girl, and lending you a little cheer, day by day. I was in London most of last week, buried in the Record Office, buying some new clo' to replace my insufferable rags, and interviewing a N. Y. publisher, whom I never saw before, and who had written me that he had proofs and MSS. he would like me to read. This was just what I wanted, to help me pay those sick-bills! So I rejoice. My Aunt is getting strong, slowly, at Tiddington. I am going out there to-morrow, to be with her a few days. The village is not far from the borders of Bucks, so I can toss you a greeting, as it were over a hedge. Our conjoint effigies give *me* great pleasure. I hope you like 'em a bit? While I dwell on my pleasures (rather scant, in this year of grace) I must add that I am "perk'd up with majestick Pride," over Mr. Lang's *Tatler* review. I know he is a true critic, and hard to please; and I have always liked his points of view, especially the historic ones. Therefore do I thank Mr. Shorter for the fine surprise I got on opening the pages. I don't know when I have been more "tickled!"

Behold, I am a very Nuisance. But do either of you remember the play I told you of, the Delavigne translation, about the poor little Princes in the Tower? I have it now, and all ready for inspection. Shall I send it to you, and where? It would be useless to try it on any manager except one who has clever children to "boom." Let C. K. S. say the word, and the burden lights upon his most friendly shoulders. It is a new rôle for me, this of taxing my friends, even with questions. Yet,—know you of any book-dealer who would buy some privately-printed works, extinct even in America? Also, one leaflet of very great rarity, I am told? I wish I knew of some Stevenson collector, especially. I shall soon be out of this financial hole, and then my talk shall be purely pastoral again, Dora mia!

I find Bank Holiday a good day to sit indoors in. The British savage, as you would say, is not so pretty as he might be, when he diverts himself. Even Oxford is full of 'Arriet. Tell me how my dear Dr. is, over in Dublin. If luck serves, I may see him in the autumn. Love to you ever from

LOUISE AND IMOGEN.

To Margaret Haskell

OXFORD, 12 WALTON ST., *Sept. 17,* 1901.

DEAR MEG,—I must send you a postscriptum by way of a palliative to my doleful letter; for my dear old Aunty has finally got a reprieve, and is in the country walking about, and in a great state of general repair! I am standing on my head with self-congratulations. Everything else, too, has brightened up within a fortnight. Even H. R. H. Andrew Lang has been saying in print that he likes my "stuff," which is "admirably untouched by 'the modern spirit,'" to wit! We hear awful rumors of heat. . . . I hope it cannot climb hills, or ambush you elsewhere.

My Mother seems to be enjoying her solitude, her creek, and her garden. She says that the Fields are going to move into one of the Snowman houses at the harbor's end. What my lone estate will do without its guide, philosopher, and friend Elisha, I dare not forecast. Much love from us both here to all dear Haskells. Write me, sometime, another nice family chronicle. . . . *A toi à tout jamais,*

L. I. G.

To The Rev. Alexander Smellie

OXFORD, 12 WALTON ST., *Sept. 17,* 1901.

DEAR MR. SMELLIE,—How good of you to send me such a nice note from Perth! particularly when I have been so bad. It was appreciated: and that is especially true of the affectionate reference to our national affliction.[1] It is a comfort, at such a time, to be among "true English hearts," as Drayton calls them, and see everywhere almost as much sympathy and fellow-feeling shown, as if one were at home. It is a terrible, an inscrutable thing. Less happy than you, I never saw the poor President. His successor, however, Mr. Roosevelt, I know and admire. He is a great book-lover, a Harvard man, and only about 42, which seems young for the head of a nation which has no hereditary honours. He has every gift except, perhaps, deliberation. Do give our dear Republic your prayers. Yes! I am yet in Oxford: anchored, as it were, in her weedy streams. After nearly five months of dangerous and exhausting illness, my dear Aunt is almost entirely well. She was so anxious to go housekeeping that we gave up, about three weeks ago, our Ship Street lodgings, and are most comfortably settled here, where half a house (a house of goodly size) is at our disposal. I have a pretty little study, and we find life as merry as sleigh-bells. Meanwhile, my fine tinsel dreams of going here and there, have faded! You see the £.s.d. loved doctors better than poeticules. When I ache for Magellan's or Stanley's adventures I trot down the tow-path to Sandford. Next

[1] The assassination of President McKinley.

month, I am going up to London, for sordid reasons, chiefly: clo', and dentists, and things. But if I can get the University Press to print my long-brewing edition of Vaughan, I shall be glad enough to be here thro' the winter. After all, Oxford lacks few beauties. The sea is one, and the hills, *real* hills, is nine!

"O the little less, and how much it is!"

(Lo, I am an ingrate, and dare not look Sir Thomas Bodley in the eye.) So you see that I am hardly likely, alas and alas! to see you quite yet on your own heather. I had a sly scheme of getting my invalid to Norfolk, a month ago, to be "braced." Not a bit of it: she wouldn't budge! I have my bicycle here, and begin to rotate. Mother is by the briny deep, and very very well. I long to get her here with me.

Somehow, I do wish you had sent me the savage Scotsman! I never mind barks and bites. And another Scotsman, Mr. Andrew Lang (whom I don't know personally) has been saying the most bee-yutiful things about that same curiously singled-out *Inquirendo,* which it is very far from meriting. Dr. Osmund Airy's monograph on Charles II, the glorious Goupil quarto, (with such pictures!) was given me by Mr. Shorter, not long ago. I am a devotee of Dr. Airy anyhow, and cannot find him (as Mr. Lang does) "hard-hearted" over my bad King. He gives him all due credit for his philosophy, his gentleness, and his love of the open air. The whole biography is a triumph, yet the breath of it is not sweet. *Corruptio optimi!* Thwarted growths always have an attraction for me, and the might-have-beens are more interesting than Sarah Duchess.

The dear Hinksons are, or were, summering at Ockley, in Surrey, where Harry has finished his "Fan Fitzgerald" (are not his stories often "rattling good" ones?) and where the Muse-petted K. T. has done two whole bookies in verse! beside preparing her Complete Poetical Works for Lawrence and Bullen. She tells me that one of the new volumes is called—charmingly don't you think?—*The Children at the Farm,* and is to be published very shortly. I have lost track of her for the last few weeks, but should not wonder if the family were now visiting in Ireland. I do hope the wee laddie is growing more robust? Pray bespeak Mrs. Smellie's friendliest thought for your friend and hers,

LOUISE I. GUINEY.

To Gelett Burgess

12 WALTON ST., OXFORD, *Dec. 6,* A. D. 1901

VERY DEAR SIR,—Weren't you nice to send me your Poetical Works? They come before a prejudiced jury; so to clear my head, after I had read 'em all through, I posted 'em to Herbert Clarke, the best and severest critic I ever knew. Now he writes: "such good stuff, Burgess! I want to keep it awhile." Hold up your head, young man, and chin side uppermost. I still like, as I always liked, the Renaissance best; then the Cognoscenti, and—Willy: I adore Willy; and the Ballade of Conceits, and the unholy Effeminates, and—what's the use of catalogues? Three of the finest of the serious staccati come close together: I mean Fog in the Cañon, In my Dreams I Flew, and The Four Elements. I hope the bookie has luck. Its form and color and slender height make up, between them, a most brazen and irresistible appeal to a man's pocket. Of that *diablerie* I suspect you to be "the onlie begetter."

I lead a most virtuous cloistered life in this misted Eden, working hard at my editing, and thawing out first one hand, then the other, at the fire; you know how. I see London, at long intervals, for a day or two at a time. Methought you were to be over here by this. How do you feel about Henley's wretched paper in the *Pall Mall?* I can get no one, least of all, the Balfours, to agree with me that the Henley who could utter that sordid, venomous, cheap, maundering cry of self-love is broken and irresponsible and crack-brained, and not worth one flash of honest anger. Look at the long, flopping, pointless sentences, the garrulous foot-notes. Is that Henley, whose phrases used to be like a highwayman's whip? It is a very sickening exhibition, but as it means mere death and decay, I can't see the valour of bringing R. L. S.'s knightly name into such a field as this, or against such a foe. I do hope his family feel the thing beneath their notice, and have had no pain from it. Pray give my love and a merry Christmas in due season, will you? to Mrs. Strong. And so fare you well, and all good attend you; and take the thanks of

Yours as ever,
LOUISE I. GUINEY.

To Mary A. Tenney[1]

12 WALTON STREET, OXFORD, *New Year's Eve*, 1901.

MY DEAR SISTER TENNEY,—Behold me kissing your inventive hand. I love that bit of green and white elegance, and am wearing it to shreds as fast as ever I can. I don't know how you hit upon a thing I needed, but you did; and if you had not done so, I should still have taken much delight in your own creation and in the all too kind thought which inspired it and sent it over sea. It came Christmas morning, with *The Tory Lover* from Miss Jewett, and other nice Americana. Believe me thankful from my heart. I am rich this week in B. P. L. letters; the Chief's,[2] Mr. Lee's, Sister Rollins', and Alice Jordan's. Pray tell the first that his dear old signature "Yours affectionately," capped exquisitely a philippic of my own. I had been complaining (in chaste female ears, mind!) of the silly stand-offish ways of English men and women towards each other; and anything of that sort has to be pretty marked before it strikes this bat! And I was parading the American Idea, in a land where all the men seem scared to death of you, save one or two owdacious original geniuses, like poets, Celts, and cranks. Said I: Now none of 'em, writing to you, would wind up as Yours affectionately? Quite right; they'd never think of such déshabille. Then I crowed. "We do those things up to the hilt; it's part of our game. And isn't it fine,"

---

[1] Of the Boston Public Library.

[2] Edward B. Hunt, head of the Catalogue Department.

I says. Then I went home, and found the document of E. B. H. afore-mentioned.

What an everlasting lot of tribulation I bequeathed to you, out of mine ignorance or heedlessness, in those Tracts-for-the-Times cards! And you not only forgive, but present embroidered collars to them that persecute! I believe from the bottom of my soul, and always did believe, that a worse heifer than L. I. G. never got into the civic china-shop. Apart from the Chartularies, and possibly the Miracle Plays, small good did I ever do, whatever were my pious intentions, to the B. P. L. which for two years supplied me with choice companionships and carbonic acid gas.

We have mud here unexcelled in quality. You saw off the bottom flounce, and carve out your shoes, whenever you return from a stroll. You really don't know, out of Oxfordshire, what mud is. But then dust has, *per contra,* no existence. I get to London now and then, generally for a little extra-parochial grind; I work hard, but wax fatter and fatter. I beg you to wish a Happy New Year, for me, to joint and several who are accessible from your daily orbit, if you lean this way or that. And may MCMII, (if he be half as genteel as that looks,) sit like a wreath of roses on your own shapely head. Goodnight, Damozel, with love from your faithful

GUINEY, LOUISE IMOGEN.
Americans in Oxford.
Needlewomen in this Library.
Vanity in Dress. *See* Life,
Moral. Collars.
Yankadoo. Manners & Customs.

To The Rev. Alexander Smellie

12 WALTON STREET, OXFORD, *New Year's Eve,* 1901.

MY DEAR MR. SMELLIE,—It was monstrous kindly of you to write, and send me your latest bookie. Be sure that I appreciate that "old Scots theology." In fact, despite an unusually busy week, I have made out already to read all in the Appendix, and your very beautiful Introduction. It is especially delightful to have Guthrie's own vivid and picturesque phrasing deployed at the foot of the page. I cannot but believe that had the edition been meant for the American market, you might have left one-half of them in the text. Seventeenth-century English is still such good current usage in our brand-new Republic! as you know. It is a possession which I hope we may not soon forfeit. Many cordial thanks for the gift. I was made very proud this Christmas by several authors' and editors' gifts of the sort. Is not Mrs. Hinkson's collection well-chosen? Her art is a standing wonder to me. It seems as if nothing so innocent was ever before so efficient. Of all the idyllic things, this which you and Mrs. Smellie propose of my visiting you with Katharine and Harry (who love you as much as I do), is the most idyllic. I cannot but fear it is much too nice ever to come true. Our plans, my Aunt's and mine, are very unsettled. Mother seems to wish me to spend next summer at home, help her adjust things there (we have to sell one house and rent another), and then return, if I choose, which I should choose if she will come over also. So far, I have no notion how things are likely to turn out, nor whether I shall be rich enough for journeys and circumnavigations.

Yes, I work along always on Vaughan. My collaborator, Miss Morgan, now in Exeter, has more to do than I have; and as the biographical researches are curiously difficult, I give a good deal of my time to helping her, even doing periodical grinds at the Br. Museum and Record Office in London. We shall have comparatively little to show for protracted labour in that direction. One thing we are greedy to do, and that is to track the whereabouts of the papers, etc., of Sir Robert Moray, a great man in his day, though a faded name in ours. We have made inquiries, in numberless instances, but so far vainly. Sir Robert was first President of the Royal Society, and Secretary of State for the Kingdom of Scotland under Charles II, besides being director of that King's laboratory, and one of the profoundly good men of the bad time. He died in 1673 in London, and is buried in the Abbey; but I have never been able to find his will. Well, Henry Vaughan's twin-brother Thomas (ob. 1666) had Sir Robert Moray for his greatest friend; and Henry says, in an unpublished letter to his cousin John Aubrey the antiquary, which is here in the Bodleian, that T. V. had "left all his papers and MSS to Sir Robert Moray." It is really these that we are after, hot-foot! Said T. V. was a very autobiographical sort of a person, kept diaries, etc. From one small commonplace-book of his in the Sloane MSS., strayed thither I know not how, we have gathered more direct and useful items than from any other one source. Now, would you, by any chance, among your learned Scots, know of any who could put us on Sir Robert Moray's trail? I do not even know whether he has descendants, or ever had a child, though he married a daughter of Lord Balcarres. Anthony à Wood, usually accurate enough, says that he died a bachelor and a "woman-hater." Pray forgive this long digression!

We rather envy you the snow. Our lot is eternal mud. I took a little nine-mile round last week, chiefly over footpaths, and my boots deserved better than ever Tom Coryat's did, so far as evidence of hard travel is concerned, to be hung up in the parish church for the edification of posterity. Oxford mud can never be brushed, but must be hewn, or sawed, off. It is of a most resolved and purposeful temper. This is New Year's Eve, and the best of all times in which to wish mundane furtherance and the Divine blessing to you, Mrs. Smellie, and your dear babes. *Faustus sit annus!* My Mother would pray so with me, were she here. "More power," too, to your manifold literary projects. (I wonder at the grace with which you can do so much, outside the labour in the Vineyard, which cannot be light.) Believe me,

Affectionately yours,
LOUISE I. GUINEY.

To The Rev. J. W. Irvine

12 WALTON STREET, OXFORD, *19 January*, 1902.

DEAR CANON IRVINE,—At the Bodleian, yesterday, I looked through carefully, the only edition (1837)

which it possesses of Ingram's *Memorials;* Littlemore Chapel is certainly not there, among all those beautiful prints. I must tell you what popped into my head as I walked home that misty evening, while my good angel climbed the hill with a big star blinking on his breast; and that is the entire conviction that we cannot be satisfied, Mrs. Irvine and I, with a magazine article only. No, Sir: with all respect, you must write a book! It would not be possible to crowd all the splendid material you have, all the portraits and plans and fac-similes you can so easily gather, into any mere magazine article. But the best of these, condensed, and welded together, would, I know, be most acceptable to the *Century*. Now please do brace up to the big task, as well as to the little one. It ought to be done; and nobody else can do it half so well. I wonder if you would let me do a stroke or two of the preparatory work, especially as that will cause me literally no trouble at all? One is, to copy out for you, on my own typewriter, which I have here, such of those precious letters as you will need to quote: and to do it so that you can insert these in your MS. for the printer, and never need allow further handling of the originals. I can promise you accurate transcripts. Then, in case you have not at hand the *Dictionary of National Biography,* would you like me to take down, some day when I am at the Bodleian, a short summary of the careers of Bloxham, Copeland, Williams, Dalgairns, Lockhart, St. John, etc.; of any persons, in short, who are intimately connected with Newman at Littlemore, from

1836 to 1846? (In fact, there is nothing I won't do to weed and plough the garden, if only you will plant the seed!) And it will be wonderfully improving and bracing to your new curate to let him bear all the parish burdens for a while, until that Book shows above the ground. What do you say to all this? It is plainly ordained, is it not? If you have not yet written Mr. Meynell, he would be an excellent person to ask about Mr. Wilberforce's original of the Richmond portrait, 1844, of J. H. N.; the large print which you have in your study, and which I have, is only from the engraving of that original, made two or three years later, and adorned with the Oratorian collar.

Pray tell Mrs. Irvine that I shall return soon the exquisite little story which she lent me, and that if I tease you with this sort of a "wishful" letter, I depend upon her to increase (not to soften!) the teasing. And with kindest remembrances to you both, I am,

Most sincerely yours,
LOUISE I. GUINEY.

To Wilfrid Meynell

12 WALTON ST., OXFORD, *18 March,* 1902.

DEAR MR. MEYNELL,—As a lover, these many years, of both your Newman books, (both far away from me now,) I could not but buy, and re-read, the new red-coated Fifth edition: and this is but to tell you that my joy in the record itself, and in all its comments and parentheses, is freshened and deepened.

Various matters of late have made me think of it and you. For one thing, my friend Canon Irvine, the dear old Vicar of Littlemore, who loves Newman's blessed memory, and has many documents written by him and about him, has often talked with me of the μονη, or the "College," as it has always been called at Littlemore; and I have urged him with all my suasions to write down the great deal that he knows about those cloistered years. And as he is, in Kipling's phrase, a "limpin' procrastitute," I have sometimes wished the detailed history of the whole sojourn at Littlemore, its plans and personalia, were, yet more fittingly, in your hands. Which brings me to the second cause of my bothering you with a letter: and that is this. Is it not the greatest pity in the world that we Catholics should never have given so much operative love and thought to that very shrine which you have had pictured opposite p. 32, that it might be bought or leased, and kept as it should be? At least ought we, I think, to get possession of the quarters of the "grave old lady," (p. 48,) a decent person, Mrs. King, since these are Newman's own rooms; and eventually, ought not the whole historic "range of stabling" to become ours, by all that gratitude and reverence mean? I have had this thing on my mind, or rather, next my heart, for ever so many years; and for the last six months, it has been a sort of obsession! How can I speak of it, or what can I, a stranger, and a shy stranger, do? except to further, with a puny might, some one who knows and can, like you, and would be willing to broach the matter to the public, in the hope and intent of reaching, not the public at all, but the fit and few? For only the enthusiasts, the Reunionists, would care very much to save those lowly walls for posterity. What do you think, Mr. Meynell? There must be others besides me who would wish to further such a project by giving towards it more than they can possibly afford! And there must be other Guineys—they spelled it so, capital letter and all, in the seventeenth century—which would come up a thousand strong, as *mine* would desire to do. It really cannot be an impracticable or even difficult project, in the right hands? If you like the suggestion, or can use it, pray forget that it came from me.

I trust Mrs. Meynell makes out to keep well, and to fight homesickness? May it be possible for her to stay a little while with our best Bostonian Mrs. Fields, who, along with many another rare quality, has the grace to be the High Chief Meynellite of U. S. A.! Please commend me to Monica; the younger children would not remember me. (I do not fail to remember them, with their radiant Florentine faces!) With all cordial good wishes, believe me ever

Faithfully yours,
LOUISE I. GUINEY.

To Dora Sigerson

ROCKLANDS, TRAMORE, WATERFORD, *20 May*, 1902.

DEAREST DORA,—It was lucky you made yourself my banker! I have had nothing but worry and trouble since I left you. The weather in Ireland has been beyond words abominable; and my Aunt has been very ill abed the whole time. She caught a chill (entirely owing to her own imprudence, as she was in first-rate condition) and had a fine collapse. I am going up to Dublin for Monday,[1] feeling wholly unfit, and more used-up from lack of sleep, &c., than any "performer" has a right to be! I don't know yet when we shall start home: probably June 5th or 6th. If my Aunt is pretty well by then, she can go on from Paddington to Oxford alone, and I can stay two or three days with you, and not cross the threshold of the accursed British Museum! But if she is still feeble, despite all our kind friends are doing for her, I can't stop in London at all. At any rate, I will drop you an elegant and commodious post-card as soon as I really know. We passed only that one night in Dublin and were off in the morning. I missed your father, as lectures were on at the Royal University, but Mrs. McGinnis and Hester kept us to an early lunch at the old house, where I was so conscious of all the changes (even Bran!) that the lump wouldn't leave my throat. Hester has changed too; but she looks happy. It was such a pleasure to see her. The sea is lovely, these days of cloud and wind: but somehow I miss my cloister cell at Oxford. With affectionate remembrances to Mr. Shorter, and also to all bills, fins, and paws under your governance, I am, dear Dora,

Yours much and ever,

L. I. G.

[1] To lecture.

To Bertram Dobell[1]

OXFORD, *June 26,* 1902.

DEAR MR. DOBELL,—You are most kind. The Sismondi is the very edition I want, and I am delighted to have your gift of the little Goldsmith. (Your adoption of that square green format flatters me, rather than my publisher, for it was I who invented, and he who accepted.) Was there ever in the world such a Goldsmithian blunder as this which you and Mr. Quiller-Couch have unravelled? Maeterlinck says somewhere that a man attracts to himself his own events, the events that are like him: I think this a darling instance of it, loving Goldsmith's genius at every point as I do. There is no immediate haste, you know, about Hurrell Froude. Thank you so much for the Traherne permission, as for the book. What a perfect day! and how full of boding and regret.

Faithfully yours,
L. I. GUINEY.

To Wilfrid Meynell

12 WALTON STREET, OXFORD, *6 July,* 1902.

DEAR MR. MEYNELL,—If all goes well here I shall get to London on the 21st. I trust that will not be too late for me to catch you in town. Meanwhile I shall go over to Littlemore, find out who owns the *μονη* now, and broach our matter to the Vicar, who is a kind friend of ours. Of course, there must be a memorial

[1] A well-known London bookseller, poet, and editor of seventeenth-century poets, including Traherne and William Strode.

to Fr. Dominic too. . . . I should think about £6 would provide a well-cut marble in Fr. Weale's Church at Reading, which is on the very site of the Abbey glorious of old. Whatever the inscription, it should end with your own phrase: "blessing England with his dying breath." Brasses are better than marbles, don't you think? but they are dependent on human care for their brightness and legibility, while marbles are not so. I shall send you my address before I start. It will be a great pleasure to me to see you and Mrs. Meynell again.

Faithfully yours,
L. I. GUINEY.

To Gwenllian E. F. Morgan

[1902.]

. . . About superstitions . . . A popular religion, old as the race, almost, clung to and grown about by the common people, must necessarily be misconstrued to some extent at all times and by some individuals, groups, or even nations: *e.g.*, we English-speaking Catholics consider the Italians superstitious; all Orientals are so; most Irish and Welsh are. Superstition, after all, is too much faith, an excrescence on true faith . . . the Reformers never in the world measured it unexaggeratedly or checked it legitimately, as the Council of Trent did, but brought it forward as a pretext and a catchword when they were set on destroying the POETRY and ROMANCE of Catholicism. The Church really did, and does, intend that blessed palms, ashes, candles, water, etc., should have a special accidental objective value, apart from their symbolism; her liturgies express this in passing, and all R. C.'s are brought up to believe it, and never treat these things breathed upon and blessed by Holy Church without reverence. . . . You can see how easy it is for certain minds to go too far. . .

The Reformers did away ruthlessly with all the touching and beautiful "sacramentals"; not one did they spare save the royal sacring, as you say, and that only because it was royal. They wanted everything prosy and practical, so they called the immemorial loveliness of ritual "fuss," and flung it away. . . .

To Wilfrid Meynell

57 S. JOHN'S ROAD, OXFORD, *Aug. 18,* 1902.

DEAR MR. MEYNELL,—In this post you will find the two books you kindly let me carry off from your Study; and very interesting they are, especially Fr. Lockhart's. I leave the dog's-eared pages "unrestored." Please accept my cordial thanks.

You will see by the superscription that we have just moved. Scarcely can I wait until October, to see those youths of Oxford who will take the new Memorial in hand. Should we not have also, from the very beginning, one or two strong names to steer by? My own choice would be Lord Halifax, and Mr. Wilfrid Ward. I think, on the whole, the thing should be (perhaps exclusively?) in lay hands, to keep it truly neutral and free. The moment you start on your little Reading brass, will you let me know? and by hook or crook, you shall have a guinea of Guiney.

Yours ever, with best wishes,

L. I. G.

57 S. JOHN'S ROAD, OXFORD, *20 August,* 1902.

MY DEAR CANON IRVINE,—It gave me great pleasure to fulfil, or try to fulfil, your little request, to-day. I would have done so yesterday, but we have been moving, and have just taken a tiny house with a good garden, on "the wrong side of the Woodstock Road." I was really obliged to spend part of this afternoon at the Bodleian, so your bit of a commission came only as an added delight. Now the only Life of Cleopatra not pure romance which I can find is an untranslated one of Giulio Landi's: *Vita di Cleopatra,* Leeds, 1796, the press-mark being 2745. f. 5. As for the English poem, alas! I distinctly remember one on the subject, beginning

"I am dying, Egypt, dying! ebbs the crimson life tide fast,"

in an old book which my father had used in his school-days. It was of Epes Sargent's editing, and entitled *The Standard Speaker.* It is not in the Bodleian. Then I tried to find a good American anthology called *Famous Single Poems,* (meaning verses of high quality written by persons who had published practically nothing else) and that isn't in the Bodleian, though I am quite sure it must contain the stanzas I mean, the only serious ones I ever met with in English which have Cleopatra for subject. But my hope is that I may possibly find them tomorrow. Meanwhile, I have already written home to have them copied, if the wait be not too long?

I have begun work in earnest on my Hurrell Froude book, and quite lately, ran across an item which perhaps you will find as interesting as I did. The Rev. Peter Maurice, (a gentleman non-Tractarian in the extreme, in fact quite Kensit-like,) says that Littlemore Church was the first one in England, since the Reformation, to be consecrated with a stone altar, and he adds that the altar and the Church, as originally designed and built, were the work of Hurrell Froude! He had a great turn for architecture. But I always had the impression (from Newman's Letters, Vol. II.) that T. Mozley drew up the plans. Is not said Rev. Peter Maurice mistaken?

We are in great confusion here, so far, and waiting for even carpets and shades. I hope you have at Torquay the sun which in Oxford seems to be a permanent absentee. My cordial remembrances to,—may I call her so?—dear Mrs. Irvine. If I succeed with my quest after the long-nosed lady who wrecked Mark Antony, I shall report at once. If you hear nothing, I shall be hanging my head, in a corner, out of my sense of unserviceableness to you. And I am always and notwithstanding,

Faithfully yours,
LOUISE I. GUINEY.

To Clement Shorter

57 S. John's Road, Oxford, *Aug. 28,* 1902.

Dear Mr. Shorter,—You are always good to me. But I fear I am "not in it" in regard to the Gosse article, anyhow, so I have no quills to rear against Isbister. You see I am up to the neck, now, in Hurrell Froude, and—domesticity. We have taken a little house! It is in *puris nat.,* so far: we have one rug, some plates, a pair of Witney blankets, and a hammer. Also a ringdove. Just now I can give very little attention to what Mr. Dooley calls "litthrachoor." But I have but a month's leeway to do the Froude book in. Possibly by early October, certainly in late October, I shall get to town.

I don't know how you can think I ever had "a dull evening" where Dora and you are; but I was so very sorry to see you tired and feverish, that I wished myself out of the way, and you be-toddied and asleep. I hope Dora is getting real benefit from her long stay in Vaterland. My best love to her when you write. Tell her that Miss Morgan covered herself with glory last week, reading two much-praised papers before the Cambrian Archæological Association at Brecon.

Yours as ever,
L. I. Guiney.

To Clement Shorter

57 S. John's Road, Oxford, *Aug.,* 1902.

My dear Mr. Shorter,—You may have known well (when you propounded such a thing), how particularly glad I should be to earn two extra guineas, in these mad centripetal days of setting up a house! But I won't take advantage of you by sending the only poem I have, when you might want to throttle it at sight! If after I tell you that it is a double-decker (*i. e.,* two tiny lyrics under one title), and purely philosophical, you can possibly want it, I shall post it along with all alacrity. To be frank, I have kept it by me about a year because I believed nobody would like it but myself. You know I write practically no verse.

About the books: the big Vaughan . . . I have long laid by, but shall have it ready in the Spring; the little prose Vaughan is to come out, I believe, by Michaelmas: it is to be in some devotional shilling series which Frowde has in hand. The Hurrell Froude book is the Longmans' affair, and will be on the market, I believe, in November. I have it in hand, but have to go slowly, the copying is so bothersome. You know more than two-thirds of it is a reprint: not only of R. H. F.'s own stuff, but of everything of moment ever written of him, friendly or unfriendly. I have sheets of some of the books, to cut up, but I can't pay for 'em all, so down I sit to grind at copying in the Bodleian! I fancy there is nothing in all this for you to make a paragraph of. I have just had such a cordial invitation from Froude's niece, the Baroness von Hügel at Cambridge (whom I never saw), to come to them early in October term-time. I shall so gladly do this, if I can; for a dozen reasons. Give old Dora a Welcome Home for me, next week.

Yours affectionately,
LOUISE I. GUINEY.

To Gwenllian E. F. Morgan

OXFORD, *9 October,* 1902.

. . . Professor Napier took us over Merton [College], into the most secret nooks of the Library, into the Fellows' Garden over the old City wall, and to the top of the tower. It was a heavenly day, pure blue overhead, opalescent cloud and haze all along the horizon on the hills, and every grove and quad below dazzlingly brilliant in scarlet, gold-green, and purple; and a thousand pinnacles stood up among them like an angelic army's spears. There never was such a city, except "Jerusalem which is above, which is our Mother!" . . . I thought all day of poor Lionel,[1] who loved it too.

In the evening, though with some reluctance, I went to the tercentenary reception at the University Galleries. . . . Everybody was there, and the scene exceptionally brilliant, with the splendid show of University gowns. . . . Dr. Garnett was there in a corner, as modest as ever. There was a most gorgeous copper silk gown floating about, with very wide fur-trimmed sleeves, absolutely mediæval, from the Sorbonne. . . .

To Gwenllian E. F. Morgan

1902.

. . . I think seriously of going to Birmingham . . . to call upon Dr. Ryder, (with whom I have had some correspondence,) at the Oratory there. He is a charming old priest, and a true poet, and was New-

[1] Lionel Johnson had died on the 4th of October, as the result of a street accident six days earlier.

man's house-mate and intimate for many years. This because I am so baffled here in Devon about Hurrell Froude! It would seem as if that entire family, distinguished as they were seventy years ago, had vanished without a sign or memorial, and "the place that knew them knows them no more": I mean so far as their old haunts are concerned. I have found at Dartmouth the pathetic graves,—so many died in their youth,—but nothing else, beyond printed records. Of course I am only at the beginning of a search. The present Mr. Hurrell Froude knows even less than I do. It is my theory that women treasure up souvenirs and recollections of one beloved more than men do, do they not? and so I mean to try to reach Mr. W. H. Mallock some day, as he was the son of Hurrell Froude's only sister. But also, I hope to be allowed to find some traces of Newman's "dearest" at the Oratory. Newman was one of the most loyal rememberers who ever lived. . . .

To Clement Shorter

57 S. JOHN'S ROAD, OXFORD, *Oct. 10,* 1902.

DEAR MR. SHORTER,—How good you are to me! Of course I am greatly inclined to say that I will do the Hazlitt, if they really want it.[1] But I could not attend to it, or make any beginning at it, before next August at earliest, say, as my hands are so full meanwhile. Would that be all right? And again, might I draw upon my own old essay on W. H. in my Little

[1] Dr. Robertson Nicoll, editor of the English Men of Letters series, had asked Mr. Shorter to obtain L. I. G.'s consent to write Hazlitt's Life for the series.

English Gallery, 1894? It is surely unknown over here; and I have said some things there which I am afraid I can say over in no better way, though I can greatly broaden their application. If you can obtain for me these two indulgences, that of time and that of text, I think you have me nailed for a book of the new series.

I wonder if you want this? I was about to send it; it is a paraphrase from Virgil (AEn. Lib. vi.). How is dear Dora? She will grieve, as I do, for our poor Lionel Johnson. Has anyone noted that the circumstances of his death are quite the same as Poe's? It is heart-breaking to have a winged creature end so, in the mire. I saw little of Lionel, but we were great friends: he had always been the contemporary most after my own heart, and I shall miss him from the world, if I live a thousand years. Many, many thanks to you.

Affectionately yours,

L. I. G.

To Wilfrid Meynell

57 S. JOHN'S ROAD, OXFORD, *13 Dec.,* 1902.

DEAR MR. MEYNELL,—Mr. Kylie came yesterday, and we "confabbed" and agreed that you were a Nice Person. He is to reconnoitre and report. Thank you so much for your *Tablet* "feeler." (I had been long wondering what possible and unsuspected spirit on the *Tablet* staff could be guilty of those animated Notes!) It would cover me with gratitude, could you have half-a-dozen slips sent me of that page? It is the document of the preliminary campaign, perfectly worded.

MISS GUINEY

FROM A PHOTOGRAPH TAKEN IN BOSTON IN HER THIRTY-SECOND YEAR

It was a shock to me to see that Fr. Bowles had died: I had set my heart on getting him here to tell us which rooms at the Monastery were the Chapel, the Refectory, etc., and in which Fr. Dominic dried himself by the fire. Do you know? Otherwise, I fear we have lost the tradition: alas and alas. You approve, do you not, of having not only a Newman, but a complete Oxford Movement Memorial Library (if only we can get it!) at Littlemore? I hope all goes well with your work and you at Bexhill.

Ever yours,
L. I. GUINEY.

To The Rev. J. W. Irvine

57 ST. JOHN'S ROAD, OXFORD, *18 January,* 1903.

DEAR CANON IRVINE,—I have been wishing for long to write you, and felt so sorry that the New Year had begun, and gone far on, while as yet I have never sent any greeting to Mrs. Irvine and to you. But I have had a very sad time of it. My poor dear Aunt died last month, almost suddenly. She had a paralytic stroke, which affected only the right arm, but she sank into a lethargy, and lived only nine days after. She had been quite as usual up to that. My Mother and I laid her to rest at Wolvercote, as she, like myself, wished not to be carried from the place where it had pleased God to let her die. It is a lifelong loss to me. We loved each other dearly, and I have so few relatives to love. She had been quite a wreck for two years, and very far from her best natural self when you saw her. Izaak

Walton's beautiful phrase, at the end of his *Life of Donne,* has been haunting me, when I am calm enough to listen to it: . . . "a small quantity of Christian dust. But I shall see it reanimated."

I must go from my grief to another topic, which has been often in my mind. You will perhaps remember what Mr. Meynell said, at the end of his column of paragraphs, when Fr. Bowles died, about the College at Littlemore? that it would be well to turn it into a sort of museum of Newman things, etc.? The very week after (I laid this *Tablet* by also to send you, but someone took it) he had another paragraph, adding that advices received from Oxford made it seem likely that the project mooted could be put through, etc. Now Mr. Meynell is as nice as ever he can be, and really full of tact; but I did think this a wee bit journalistic, as the scheme (which was mine, though not matured) was stated wrongly, to begin with; and as *nothing whatever* had been done about it, first or last. For of course I felt that you were the very first person I wished to consult. This was one reason why I was sorry not to have seen you for so long, nor to have answered your delightful letter about the new Window and other pleasant topics. My idea would be to suggest public interest only in the two rooms at the end, old Mrs. King's rooms, which were occupied by J. H. N., if you thought well of it: to turn them into a little Oxford Movement Library, where all the books by, or about, that whole *generatio quaerentium Deum,* could be gathered in and kept. Far from having it a Newman collection only, I should like to take in even Pattison's, J. A. Froude's and all, the management to lie with a small committee chosen equally from your Church and mine. I had thought of asking Lord Halifax and Mr. Wilfred Ward to head it. I am sure they would. But you must decide, as you will, for me. What do you think? It might be of unique interest and value as a historical landmark for Anglican and "Roman" alike. My love always to Mrs. Irvine.

Yours very faithfully,
LOUISE I. GUINEY.

To Wilfrid Meynell

57 S. JOHN'S ROAD, OXFORD, *Jan. 19,* 1903.

DEAR MR. MEYNELL,—I feel as if I owed you some sort of an apology, though I am innocent enough. Mr. Kylie tells me that Mr. Justice Walton's son has just told him, at the Union, that the Vicar of Littlemore had written to the *Tablet,* disclaiming any knowledge of a scheme for a Newman Memorial there, and objecting to it on the ground that it would deprive him of rent-producing property. This is a dreadful muddle. It reflects obliquely upon you, and it must look to you as if I was—well, at least, a person not distinguished by prudence and accuracy. The truth is this. Absolutely nothing had been done, when, following up your first attractive mention of the matter when Fr. Bowles died, you added, the week after, that "advices from Oxford made it seem probable," etc. But I suppose it must have looked to the dear old Vicar as if his dearest interests were being attacked. Now, though my scheme was not to have the $\mu o \nu \eta$ bought at all but to have J. H. N.'s two rooms in it hired (and at a somewhat better rent, too, than old Mrs. King now pays for them), and though Canon Irvine was the very person of all others whom I most wished to consult, it has happened that I never went up to Littlemore to broach the subject, because I have had so much domestic affliction, especially since December set in. My dearest Aunt Betty died on the 28th and her mind had begun to fail some time before. It is a very heavy grief to me, and has quite de-railed, so to speak, my work and my world. But I am so sorry about this Littlemore matter. I know Canon Irvine well enough to feel sure I shall be forgiven also in that quarter, and that the little Memorial can yet be properly launched with his full connivance and goodwill. Meanwhile, for your own complete vindication, pray tell the *Tablet* people how it all came to pass. And don't hate me! I should not like to be thought insensible of all your most friendly courtesy. I hope the *magnum opus* was finished at Bexhill?

Ever faithfully yours,
LOUISE IMOGEN GUINEY.

To Dora Sigerson

57 S. JOHN'S ROAD, OXFORD, *Jan. 19,* 1903.

DEAREST DORA,—I have been through the deep waters since I wrote you last. My dear Aunt's mind began to fail in November. She never cared much for any one but me, and in the end followed me like my shadow. But I could not cheer her, nor do much for her; we just suffered together. She had a sudden paralytic stroke on Dec. 19, and sank at once into a lethargy, lived nine days, and, without any pain, went Home three days after Christmas. Well, I am doing my best, turning to the great refuge of hard work, and not wearing black; but they are long, long days and nights. K. T. H. told me the Dr. was visiting you, or was about to visit you. My love to him. My Mother is very well indeed, and keeps her old affection for you. My best thanks this late for the dear little Christmas memorandum-book, a pocket treasure.

Ever yours,
L. I. G.

To Wilfrid Meynell

57 S. John's Road, Oxford, *Feb. 5,* 1903.

My dear Mr. Meynell,—Many thanks for your note. The "Newman Memorial" is a deadlock. I have only myself to blame that I failed to sound Canon Irvine in the beginning. You see, I spoke to you about it, for advice, as soon as the idea struck me, and before it was formed; and then, I spoke to no other person whatever, until the bubble was pricked. Prolonged domestic trouble, my dear Aunt's sad mental condition, and her sudden death, kept me from going up to Littlemore; I had no energy for it, and put it off until too late. I thought nothing could well be more tactful and graceful than all you have said in the *Tablet,* first and last; yet had I known, or seen in the proof, the little announcement that operations had really begun, I should, of course, have talked with Canon Irvine before it could get into print. For he was the person of persons whom I wished to consult. But now he is quite set against the scheme. I have explained fully that the whole thing was projected upon a historic, literary and "non-sectarian" basis, and that Anglicans must of necessity be the majority, both in establishing the Library, and in controlling it. All in vain: with the most forgiving and even affectionate attitude towards me, as ever, he keeps on repeating that he "cannot give any foothold to the "Romans" in Littlemore Parish"! It seems quite hopeless. He offers to take religious care of any Newman or Oxford Movement treasures confided to him for keeping; but that is the whole extent of his capitulation. And if *he* could live for ever, dear soul, that would not be a theory absurd in the application. So I can do nothing further. I have lately laid the matter before the University Chaplain, Canon Kennard, a confirmed Newmanite. He is full of interest, and offers to go up and see the Vicar when it is less miry by the way. They will be sure to get on; they are rather of a piece, and both charming; but I have my doubts of the issue. Plainly, nothing can be done meanwhile. I did not see the American endorsement, which must have appeared lately. Would you mind letting me know in which number of the *Tablet* it came out? I should like to get it. Mr. Kylie shall have your Tartarean message.

Yours faithfully,
L. I. GUINEY.

To Mrs. F. H. Briggs

57 S. John's Road, Oxford, *Feb. 7,* 1903.

My very dear Ada,—For your two long enchanting letters, I have been your debtor for a very long while. I fear I have not even thanked you for your Christmas gift. But you know that where I once stood towards a friend, there I stand, and that no affectionate thought like yours is ever lost upon me. Besides, I have meant to write, these many weeks, and could not get up the necessary energy. You will have heard what has happened: that my darling old Aunty has gone away. It is all very strange to me, with whom, ever since my infancy, she was all but incorporated. I suppose no person ever can have realized or appreciated another's lifelong selflessness, more than I did hers. And for all our solitary and recluse living over here, I like to think that she was really happy, and often said so, this last of all our years together. Her mind had begun to fail, owing to the terrible disease (Bright's) which, physically, she was almost able to beat down, but she was up and about to the very last; then a sudden stroke of paralysis, a week of quiet sleep, and—the Waking. It was a great mercy to me that my Mother was here. She keeps perfectly well, and has planted her tulip-bulbs to-day. We have had no snow whatever, and very little frost.

Will you not tell Mr. Church that I received his gift (a perfectly brilliant and successful thing it is), and felt most grateful both for that, and for the note from Mrs. Church and himself, which came while my grief was new? If you will do this, it will save me writing it. I am ashamed to say how I still shirk the simplest offices of friendship, though I try, daily, and with fair results, to keep up my editing work, or my researches at the Bodleian, whose beauty is like an isle of peace, and quite unapproachable among libraries. Of course I know that all this stagnant dulness is but a reaction from long and deep anxieties. So forgive it and me. I do not know Mr. Martin Harvey, nor, indeed, anybody here whom I did not know ten years ago. I like the reports of him, however, and his singularly interesting face, seen on posters, and in the weeklies. I never get to London, or the play, of late. And as I am pretty deaf, I suppose I must begin to batten instead on memories of Edmund Kean, or some such antediluvian genius. (I was once actually asked by George Riddle if I remembered Charles Kean! And I *was* young, then.) I do hope your two dramatic fledglings are proving themsleves a credit to you, dear girl.

We send you all much love. I think very often of my dear Mother Briggs. You have not told me how Fred's church get on at Sharon, or whether it is builded stone, now, and not a dream.

Yours always, Ada *mia*,

L. I. G.

To Dora Sigerson

57 S. JOHN'S ROAD, OXFORD, *Mar. 3rd*, 1903.

DEAREST DORA,—I lack an excuse to write you, but have been wanting to do so, "for very wantonness." I do hope you keep well? We are dull and quiet here, but all right; and my mother is so interested in our scrubby little garden that it does me good to see her. I am getting Oh! so fat, because I sit too much a-boddling in the Bod, and have no one to play with, out-of-doors. On Friday I was in London, rushing thither and back, and blew you a kiss from Bloomsbury. I saw no one I knew but Herbert Clarke; as I had a noon errand on Cornhill, I looked him up, and had my first sight of him since July. Between that and this, he nearly died, but I am very grateful indeed that he didn't. From a sketch I saw in (I think) *The Westminster Gazette,* I infer that K. T. H. is in Ireland now. It is a blossomy season even here. I wish you might come and see! Please tell your lord that I particularly desire him, of his goodness, to tell me the bookseller from whom he bought poor Lionel's two books for me; for I have an American order for said bookseller.

Yours always, dear Dora,
LOUISE.

To Gwenllian E. F. Morgan

7th March, 1903.

. . . I had a walk yesterday. Oxford was wonderful in all vistas, partly owing to the floods, every field a great lagoon, where the clear yellow and orange sky lay mirrored, with tumbling violet-coloured clouds riding over and through. Put those spires and pinnacles for a background; and you see the picture which "takes the heart of me" the more, the longer I live. . . .

To Clement Shorter

57 S. John's Road, Oxford, *Apr. 7,* [1903.]

Thank you very much, dear Mr. Shorter, for your kind words about my opusculum (I am really chiefly pleased to have pleased you), for the copy of the *Tatler,* and for the "art critic's" admission-card to the Historical Portrait show here. It will be a maddening sort of show to anyone who has any historical hunger and thirst, owing to the fact that too often both painter and sitter are what Wood calls "anonymall." I am glad you had Buckinghamshire air for Easter. Dora will be amused to hear that I have lately discovered two stage beauties whose photographs, at least, remind me strongly of her: Constance Collier and Marie Studholme! I have not had one holiday since Christmas, and am still lumbering along, weighed down with arrears. I got quite a heartbreaking blow last week, on hearing that Prof. Saintsbury is almost on the point of bringing out a big book of Minor Carolian Poets: a thing I have dreamed of since I was a kiddy at school: a thing I have always believed I was *for.* I suppose his men are my men: Cartwright, Quarles, Habington, Stanley, Fanshawe, Sherburne, Crompton, Rochester &c., the golden lyrists who have not come, as Herrick, Carew, Vaughan and Marvell have done, into their inheritance. WORRA! . . . I don't know when I have gone green with envy, wrath, and inner protest before! But you can't edit old poets properly on 2½d and no beer per month: that's flat. I am going into training to drink Prof. Saintsbury's health, *without* the rider: "God send this Crumb-well down."

If you have any duplicates hanging useless about your Library, the Parish Library here (in which I am intimately interested) would be overjoyed to get them and pay the carriage. Try us, some day when you are bursting with benevolence? With love to the Bird of Paradise and all her birds of earth,

Yours always,
LOUISE I. GUINEY.

To Florence Warren[1]

14 SOUTH PARADE, BATH, *April,* 1903.

. . . Your good letter came, and comforted me for Easter. I have been very low-spirited, and kept out on the hills here, by myself, all I could. . . . Fresh air is my salvation. "Nature never did betray The heart that loved her." And I am better. Mother is in great form. The waters seem to act like magic upon her, and today, in alternate snow and warm sun, she walked three miles or more with me. . . . Bath is certainly the finest city, and has the finest site, of any I know, untravelled as I am. But it does not grip the heart as Oxford does, with her "willow-haunted streams." This house has a magnificent prospect.

[1] Miss Warren of Felton, Delaware, was one of the first women students in Oxford. At the time of her death in 1917 she had completed, with glossary and notes, a translation of the *Dance of Death* for the Early English Text Society. The manuscript, which had taken some years to prepare, had to be abandoned, together with all Miss Warren's other belongings, in Magdeburg, Germany, at the outbreak of the war in 1914, and has not been recovered.

Fanny Burney once stayed in it, and gushed delightfully over it. I have not read a thing, my so-called intelligence not being equal to it; but the Spring in "good old Zummerzet" is excellent to look at. . . .

To Clement Shorter

[*About 1 May,* 1903.]

DEAR MR. SHORTER,—I owe you my best thanks yet once again. I can easily condone your being so very good to me, when I remember that you have it in you to be equally good to all the undeserving! But I should like to pick a bone with you for implying that dear Mangan was more of a "genius" than Emerson. Why? Because the latter had some sense of human and personal responsibility? And don't you really think J. C. M.'s German translations, many, or most, of them, good? I suspect Dora's liking for "Und dann nichts mehr" is no greater than mine, who would put among my reasons for liking it, its extreme faithfulness to the original. Mr. Morrow's drawing is a triumph, even to the hands. I delight in it, and wonder at it. Would you care to reproduce this? It is a faded photograph, perhaps impracticable, done in 1890 by F. Holland Day. Its interest now is that the picturesque old rambling wooden fence (all the colour of the boughs above it, and the ground beneath) has been replaced, every few rods, by an abominable corrugated iron substitute, hideously durable. So perishes the poetry of Hampstead Heath: as D. and I saw, the day we were there together. Of course you know Millfield

Lane (Poet's Lane being Leigh Hunt's name for it) and its hundred associations with Coleridge, Shelley, Hunt, and Keats. It runs by the side of Caen Wood, on the left, *i. e.,* south, as you approach the Heath from Highgate. The little ponds used to show up prettily when this old print was new. If you use it, may I have it again? And please do not pay me, if you do. It will be reward enough to see it in the *Sphere.*

We have been away three weeks in Somerset, and are newly home. We intended to "pick up," but we haven't, to any appreciable extent, and we take turns in keeping each other in bed. My mother is the gaol-bird just now, and pretty miserable she is. It all makes me fear greatly that my beloved Oxford is gey ill to live wi'. With most affectionate messages to dear Dora, I am,

Yours always,
L. I. G.

To Clement Shorter

57 S. JOHN'S ROAD, OXFORD, *19 May,* [1903.]

DEAR MR. SHORTER,—You will forgive me, I hope, if I say that I have a horror of making definite engagements of this sort, because I cannot bear to break them. But if I have to fix a date for delivering copy (*i. e.,* eggs before hatching!) I will put it as far off as possible, and then, in all likelihood, be better, as I usually am, than my word. Let us say, then, that I am to send some 45,000 words on Hazlitt, a Life in little, and an Appreciation, by May 1, 1904. *Quod Deus concedat.* Will that be agreeable to Dr. Nicoll? I do not now think that I can work over much of my old essay: it is too congested for the purpose. Meanwhile, I shall look towards some other books of the Series, in order to gauge just the sort of thing which is wanted.

You do not say whether you got my photograph of Millfield Lane, Hampstead Heath? I have cherished it long. Perhaps its interest will not be so apparent to others! With friendliest wishes always, and love to Dora the Silent, I am

Yours faithfully,
L. I. GUINEY.

To Bertram Dobell

OAK-APPLE DAY, [*29 May,*] 1903.
57 S. JOHN'S ROAD, OXFORD.

DEAR MR. DOBELL,—No matter about the books: I am so used to never being able to do what I like! My attraction towards that particular copy of that Fine Old Girl, the Countess of Winchilsea, lay just in the MS. corrections; and as you can't duplicate those, pray don't mind hunting up the book elsewhere. Thank you so very much for Strode's lovely poems. I knew him! I know most seventeenth-century English writers, and I know nothing else. The Epitaph of this group is better known than the rest: I have run aross it a dozen times, I should think, in MS. Luckily, I have preserved one reference, which you may know, or may not know: to Sloane MS. 1792, in B. M. This contains (signed W. S.) the section, "Sleepe, pritty one" and the

Epitaphium, "Happy grave." *Musarum Deliciae* has an epitaph upon a son of Dr. Prideaux, which sounds like Strode, ending well:

> "'Tis better die a child, at four,
> Than live, and die so at fourscore.
> View but the way by which we've come,
> Thou'lt say he's best that's first at home."

I have written in, in pencil, some variant readings on your p. 4. I took special interest in the Epitaph because I once made a collection of perfect old ones, which I still have by me, and never mentioned to anyone before. If I had "the mind," as Lamb observed of Wordsworth in a like ironic case, I should set up for an active member of the Bullen-Dobell Diggers' Club. So long as I shall be in Oxford, you may at any time call on me for excavations among the Rawlinson MSS., or anywhere. It would give me real pleasure. The only difficulty in one's way is that there is no indication whatever in any catalogue of the specific contents of a MS. book. There are scores in Rawl. and also Ashmole MSS., which are indicated only as volumes of poetry in handwriting of the seventeenth century, &c. Rather foggy! (You should come here for a couple of months, and take our "shanty," elegantly furnished in deal and bamboo.) I am glad to hear of the Elia Series.

With many thanks, and friendliest good wishes, I am

Faithfully yours,

L. I. Guiney.

To Bertram Dobell

28 July, 1903.

DEAR MR. DOBELL,—Your powers of knowledge and of inference may be remarkable enough: but I defy you to realise one-eighth of the rapture you provided for me yesterday! Long as I have been the bounden slave of poor old W. H., I never so much as held a letter of his in my hand before, let alone actually owning one. Of course *you* know, too, how few letters he managed to write in the course of his two and fifty years. Hazlitt arrested for debt, and Lamb in the stocks! This is a great discoverer's year, when we can spy our dearest immediate forefathers in such gay predicaments. As for thanking you, words fail me. But you are "terrible nice," and that I shall remember while this machine is to her. (Now I shall have something to work on H. E. Clarke's envy: he adores Hazlitt too.)

The Incarnatio sonnet is indeed magnificent. I think you're right about "violet" having had once a broader meaning; as I am off to "Bod." immediately, I shall look it up in the N. E. D.[1]—(No, I can't: there's no V volume yet; but the Imperial Dictionary will serve.) It is a beautiful word, vi-o-lent, quâ word. God "shining" beams is an odd use, but perfectly transparent as to meaning, and a figure in itself. What was the secret of old by which commonplace men, or fourth-rate poets, could say (could not fail to say, rather,) such "deep-mouth'd" things? It baffles one. We are a shabby generation in the face even of a single sonnet like this.

[1] New English Dictionary.

You mention *Parnassus Biceps,* 1656. I have been wanting to see that book for years. Do you own a copy? And will you lend it to me, if so, for two days next September? I am off to Yorkshire this week. If you are in want of some trusty person to do the Strode copying in Dublin, do ask T. W. Lyster, Esq., National Library, Leinster Lawn, to find you the right person; and say I put you up to it. He is a Trinity College man, the National Librarian, a friend of Dr. Grosart's, and a very good old friend of mine. Incidentally, he is ORFUL intelligent, and knows a deal about poetry. Fare you well and ever better. And believe me most gratefully and faithfully yours,

L. I. GUINEY.

To Edward A. Church

57 S. JOHN'S ROAD, OXFORD, *August,* 1903.

DEAR MR. CHURCH,—I feel that I owe you for favours manifold. Surely, I have made no indecent haste in thanking you for them? Even *Cassiopy* is now an old-time denizen of my shelves, and the delight of all the wicked "U. S. A.'s" to whom I lend her. But I do not forget, in my non-literary age, your kindness, and that of others who first do me one gracious turn after another, and then release me from all the remarks usual in polite society. To tell the truth, I can but be grateful for that, being pretty tired and inoperative, and permanently wool-headed. I could balance easily in a teaspoon all I have been able to write for the past twelvemonth. This is posted from Hinderwell in Yorkshire, whither I came a fortnight ago to whet myself on moor-scents and sea-scents. It is all very odd and quaint and endearing, this coast, and we are near the immemorial Whitby whose legends you will remember out of *Marmion*. But I am a dull baggage yet. . . . I don't feel inclined to return to my native land, though I never appreciated it more. The peace, the simplicity, the anonymity of life here, at present, are "better than rubies." . . .

Perhaps you will have seen the latest R. L. S. books, though I have not, save across the smoked glass of the reviewers: *Memories of Vailima,* and Mr. Hammerton's cleverly edited miscellany of *Stevensoniana*. And poor Henley has gone. An irreverent English friend of mine, who never liked him, dismissed him thus: "May he rest in oblivion and peace, he and his 'unconquerable soul' filched from Emily Brontë!" But why do I prate of poets and of the printed page, whose spirit is wholly engrossed with sleep, viands, clo', and nothingness? . . .

How is the dogling? I have fallen perforce from S. Bernards of ever-blessed memory, to a couple of ring-doves. They are my only diversion, unless you count in the good soul out of Somerset who keeps house for us now in Oxford, and daily makes some such remark as: "Tell I when to buy en, and us'll have en for supper." She is yclept Tutt. I urged Mam to take her, on the ground that reproof could be artistically administered, when necessary, by a mere iteration of her name. But I have missed my idiomatic aim, because she is perfect in that state of life to which it hath pleased God to call her.

Fare you well, and Save you. Commend me to your winsome lady. Believe me grateful for your untiring friendship, and always yours to keep,

LOUISE I. GUINEY.

To Mrs. J. W. Irvine

HINDERWELL, YORKSHIRE, *11 August,* 1903.

DEAR MRS. IRVINE,—Your pleasant note has just reached me, here at the moor-and-sea end of the world. It is very nice and cool and restful, but I should so much like to be with you on that lovely lawn, between the roses, and the bewitching little pigs, this afternoon! I thank you ever so much for thinking of us. Nothing but a great pressure of work, and the sudden departure of my Mother for America, in July, kept me from calling on you before I came away. We had the rather alarming news that our little country house in Maine, the only house we now own, where many of our memoried household gods are, had been broken into; and nothing would serve the Mammy but that she must rush over to see for herself. There are not many persons of her age and constitution so tamelessly energetic. I simply had to let her go, as I was not rich enough to go with her. She now writes that things are not quite so bad as she feared; and that if all goes well, she will return in October. She always regretted failing to return your kind call, when you came during the furniture interregnum, and had nothing to sit on! She had extraordinary trouble in getting a good servant, for long, and that kept her tied to the house, but at last we captured a somewhat elderly "jewel," who is now keeping house alone in our absence, and is the greatest conceivable comfort to both of us.

From the *Oxford Times,* I gather how busily dear Canon Irvine is going about; so I know that this activity means health, and am so glad of it. Have we not had a gloomy sort of summer, on the whole? This is my first visit to Yorkshire. We are lodging, and battening on mushrooms and fresh fish. My companion is my good friend and fellow-citizen (doubly, of Boston, U. S. A., and of Oxford) Florence Crocker: she who appeared once with me upon the Vicarage steps, as we were returning from a long drive, and had no watch with us, and found you in a bonnie dinner-gown, and the company and the viands respectively hungry and hot! (But you looked so pretty, we forgot our own enormities!) On the way up, we managed to see York Minster, and even Durham the all-magnificent; and we broke one journey to make a two hours' between trains call on the dear Wiltons at Londesborough. You will remember Canon Wilton's beautiful verses? They live in such an exquisite secluded place, with the most romantic historical associations. We had, all round, the best time that ever was packed into so small space. I wonder if you are going to Devon again? I have carried considerable work with me to these peaceful quarters, but feel too lazy to do much but mope and stare at the hills and the sea. The land has no trees, and the water no isles, so that the eye travels easily on long journeys. Well, all good be with you and yours. I hope to get back about September 15th, to my small cabin. Please give my affectionate remembrances to Canon Irvine. Thanking you again, I am as ever,

Very faithfully yours,
LOUISE I. GUINEY.

To Bruce Porter

HINDERWELL, YORKSHIRE, *August 12,* 1903.

MY DEAR BRUCE PORTER,—It is ever so long since you sent me those enchanting little pictures of your eyrie (how do you spell it?) on the hills; never did I see such a dream of a place, more cloud than clod. And I hear that you were ill, which set me thinking more about you, and wishing blessings on your head; though with my graceless indolence, I never wrote a line. Then, all of a sudden about a month ago, who should turn up in Oxford, about ten o'clock one rainy evening, but the old Lupe, looking far blither than ever I saw him, with his pretty sister, and a delightful young rough-shod radical of a Russo-American, whose name I forget, though it would be a dull business to forget *her*. It was fine to see him again. He told me you were over "here," with a circular gesture; but I have no definite address, so approach by way of the Golden Gate. I wish you would say how well you are? And if you're near these isles, do look me up. There are things worth while in that Oxford, which still seems to me the fittest cloister. The landscape is still, to quote your words which I retain with glee, "too bloomin' tidy," but I can take you to wild freckles of it, here and there. I am here until Sept. 10th or thereabout. No tidy tricks about Yorkshire! We have moors and sea, windmills, lighthouses, tawny sails, torrents, and never a tree. Anything queerer than the little barnacle-like fishing-villages Runswick and Staithes, on either side of me, stuck anywhere up the cracks of the reddish crags, you never saw in your life. I have my ups and downs, too, not so extreme as yours, but bad enough; and at present I am only intermittently the owner of a head. It won't work for fifty-one weeks, then it goes like mad, day and night thro' the fifty-second, and is reconverted to "nullifidianism," as my seventeenth-century folk called it. I never see a Muse or a poet. There are no literary persons allowed in Oxford! My mother is in America; she has been here, and may return. I sue her, with some faint hopes of an abduction to follow. You must tell me, for my sins, how Mrs. Strong is, and Mrs. Williams, and Miss de Fremerie? I say "for my sins," because remorse digs me for not inquiring at first-hand. I cannot goad my pen into any of the old decencies, save by taking one at a time, and once a year. There is a Scot in London named Hammerton, who has just edited a book called *Stevensoniana*: an anthology of things said of R. L. S. I haven't seen it; the menu (12s 6d) being dissuasive. But I think he is clever, and knows what's what. I put him up to asking your leave to include

"O Sailor, sailing the unfathomed Sea!"

and if he didn't write (but perhaps he did?) it was because the advice came too late to act upon. He got hold of my sonnet and the longer rhyme, somehow, after most of the book was in press. I have seen ever so many most favourable notices of the *Memories of Vailima,* especially Mrs. Strong's half. Whenever you write home, please send my love to her, and to Mrs. Williams too. I shall answer the latter's moss-grown and mildewed letter ere I die. This is a photograph of Tom Meteyard's new studio at Scituate, separate from the house: every stone of it, every shingle of it, every panel and pane of it, laid by Tom's own lily fingers! It took him æons. But it is done. He celebrated, and became genial, and gave a mediæval party; I am even informed, by an incredible innuendo of his lady-mother's, that Tom was heard to talk!

Now, fare you well, Sir, and ever better. I hope all goes well with your beloveds at home. Of my few kinsfolk, I have lost the dearest since I came to England: my great friend and lifelong companion, my poor Aunt Betty, who died in Oxford in 1902. The best of private griefs is that they "break our glass to get more light," and open our vistas, and make one friends with prior and posterior life. To gain such a citizenship is rather comforting, when you know you have made a muddle of your other opportunities in this world.

Your faithful sister and fellow,

L. I. GUINEY.

(S. John's Road, Oxford, is my permanent address, so far as I know it. We leave here in a fortnight.

Qualify "we" by dividing it into me and Florence Crocker, once of Cambridge, Massachusetts, now of the British Empire nomad and spectator.)

To Charlotte E. Maxwell

HINDERWELL, YORKSHIRE, *13 August,* 1903.

. . . An American friend and I came up here among the moors, on the coast, to pass August, when all-perfect Oxford supplies no air to the lungs she has charge of. It is romantic and quaint, and cold as Merry Christmas. Perhaps you will not have heard that my Mother is in Boston! She flew back in July, to see about our Maine Cottage, which had been "burgled," and which she is now wishing to sell. It has just been rented, and she has left it, but I have not heard as yet where she now is, except that I am sending my letter, this week, in care of Mr. Pelletier, 30, Court Street, an old pet of mine who is now a risen lawyer! She has solemnly agreed, though, under the sweat of my brow to make her, to return in October. I can't go home: it gives me the most genuine and involuntary fit of trembling to think of it, much as I long for the faces of my friends. The pace at which everything goes there, the noises, the publicity, the icicles, the mosquitoes, the extreme climatic conditions,—I am not equal to face them now; and I fall back, as on and into, a mossy bank, to the peace, the utter simplicity, the anonymity, of my life in England, and feel that I cannot give it up, and more, that I have actually some right to it. You'll both understand, and Hannah does:

but there is not a single other person in all Boston who does not half suspect I have turned Anglomaniac or what not! That numberless natives of U. S. A. live in Europe for what even I call unworthy motives is surely no reason why this poor nigger should be worried on the subject! Is it? We have a meek little house with a "bumptious" garden, and a jewel of a housekeeper, both at next to nothing a year. Oxford doesn't suit Marmee, though, and I'll live "any old where," so that the latitude means access to the Bodleian, when she returns. In London, where I know many, I should not be able to keep my cell as I do. I hope the time will come when I shall be roused out of the long lethargy, and good for all the old games.

Before I end a Perfect Pig of a letter, all about my silly self, I must answer your query about the two poems. They are both in my best book, *A Roadside Harp*, Houghton, Mifflin & Co., 1893. It does so rejoice me to learn of your golden vacation spent with your friends. May it have made up for all the worry of the summer before! I think I may have caught a fish for you in the B. P. L., in the person of an ex-colleague there, a young Mrs. Chamberlain, a widow, head of the Fine Arts Department, who lately spent several weeks in Oxford. She is all right socially, and the Gymnasium is what she would enormously like and profit by. I suppose poor dear Mrs. Fields and Miss Jewell are both still unable to return? But I am sure that Mrs. Gavin still rolls over the string, world without end: bless her smiling rotundity! Can I never do anything over here for Miss Deane and you? Give her my 'and and 'eart.

And believe me, dearest of women, yours to keep so long as you will.

LOUISE I. GUINEY.

I plunge into femaleness, of which a postscript is said to be the inevitable symbol, long enough to tell you that your bas-relief portrait, one of the joys of my life, was, though most carefully packed, smashed across the chin and cheek in coming over, in my Mother's train, last October. Alas and alas. After many makeshifts, I have so placed it, in our tiny drawing-room, that the light strikes it in a way not to reveal the fatal unmendable gashes: and nearly everybody, coming in, says, as Gelett Burgess did, a fortnight ago: "Who's your Beauty?"

To Florence A. Crocker

YORK, *Aug. 28,* 1903.

I have had such an adventurous day, my dear, that I simply can't resist telling you of it. . . .

So I caught a Bolton Percy train at 12.38. It wasn't intending to stop there on that occasion, but the guard vowed, unasked, that he'd make it stop, and stop it did. I saw the lovely village, with its thatched roofs and ancient oaks, and a pleasing epitaph in the Church (which has a most beautiful East window of ancient glass, with ten tall saints in the five lights) which commemorates the "wife" of William Mordaunt Milner, 1805. The bereaved gentleman actually forgot to name her at all, in his inscription! but he carefully states that he "lost in her the Advice of one who was endowed with a Mind capable of pointing out the right Path for his Actions, and following that Advice, he never erred"! A proper spouse, that. Next, I made for Nun Appleton, two and a half miles across the fields, under a grumpy-looking sky, colliding with calves, cobs, pheasants, turkeys, pigs, &c., and capturing mushrooms for my breakfast as I went. The park has some big oaks, survivors of Sherwood Forest. A grand modern house showed up at the end of the avenue, and I made, pack and all, for the front door, thinking to encounter another paragon of information regarding Fairfax portraits, like the flunkey at Gilling. In the porch, sewing, sat two ladies with frizzled gold hair, and a gentleman. I asked meekly if the house were shown? The elder lady, whom I "took to" at sight, answered pleasantly that it should be shown, only there was nothing in it worth looking at: and was I interested in the Fairfaxes? You bet, sez I, (only in more academic phrases,) and in Marvell too. She beamed, and told me that there wasn't a shred of anything historic on the place, that portraits, furniture, MSS. everything, was taken away when her father, Sir Angus Holden, bought out the Milners; but that Mr. Fairfax, my good Lord's legitimate heir, dwells hard by at Milborough near Copmanthorpe, and would be delighted to show anyone interested in them the tombs, memorials, &c. The gentleman, her brother-in-law, I think, turned out to be a Fairfax also, in the female line. To cut a long story short, the charitable creatures turned me into a wonderful great garden (Marvell's "Garden"!) kept me to tea, and had me driven to the station. As my blood is up, I really mean to attack the other estate, and put my shyness under foot. So as it was spitting rain, and very unpromising as to railway connections, &c., I suddenly decided to come back to York, instead of going Selbywards, and start fresh in the morning. So I trod again the boards of the Roman Cemetery, captured a pound of jolly plums for 5d at our shop, and rang up the worthy dames of Castlegate. At 9 P. M., I shall feast on hot milk and malt bread, and snuggle into the best bed in these isles. . . . With love, dear Florence, I am

Yours much and ever,
L. I. G.

To Charlotte E. Maxwell

57 S. JOHN'S ROAD, OXFORD, *14 September*, 1903.

YOU BELOVED THING,—What a delightful surprise for me, this news of yours! I do not know what I have done to deserve such a pleasure from the Immortals, that I shall really see you soon again. Of course you will come to the Mitre on Thursday! that's the place for you: and to give the

> "City of streams, and City of one stream
> Whose waves are generations."

as many days as ever you can. You will never regret it. I am newly back from Yorkshire; I went there to work, and I couldn't work; my poor head won't go;

and as I am under contract to edit a fussy book before October 10, you may judge whether or no I have to "hustle," as we say in America. But Oh! all the Stoic principle that ever was cannot keep me from asking if I may not go out and play with you when you come! You won't mind? And I shall try not to be too deadly dull. You know I am all alone in my little hut here with our good housekeeper, the Mammy being over in Maine? I shall be delighted to meet Miss Barnes. Do not forget to ask me to give you the address of the most delightful lodgings imaginable, in case you go to see the ideal Gothic Cathedral at Wells. My own great friend of years ago, also a Miss Barnes of New York (Harriet Isabella of that ilk) has just arrived in England; I am looking forward so to seeing her, later in the month. As to Mr. Emmet, his very name brings my heart up into my mouth: for I suppose there is no one in this world who worships R. E. more than I do; and next Sunday, mind you, is the hundredth anniversary of his "martyrdom for an idea." I fancy your Mr. Emmet may be a brother of Miss Kathleen Emmet, of whom I used to hear a good deal about 1894-97, when we were much with poor Mrs. Clarence Blake. So pray do bring him over, too, and keep me from paying him an ancestral idolatry, if you can! If you will but make use of me, meanwhile, in any Oxonian way you can (such as engaging rooms, or what not) I shall be "pleased as Punch." You mustn't call names, though! *I'm* no goddess: that is your sole and exclusive prerogative; and I do not know a single other goddess in the living world. Be a good Dian, and shine late and early on

Your entirely devoted shepherd swain,

L. I. G.

To Dora Sigerson

22 Oct., 1903.

DEAREST DORA,—I am so sorry to hear about poor little pretty Cuheen, and wish I were there to help cheer you up. It was such a disappointment to me not to be able to get to Ealing; and that would have been even worse, had I known you were both going out! I sat up until just before dawn, working, and slaughtering the landlady's gas. But I actually got the job done, turned it over in the morning, and fled for home. This blessed county is all under water. It is extraordinarily picturesque, and is also provocative of much local profanity, as there have been three great floods here since last Christmas. I shall be flying up to Liverpool on either Monday or Tuesday, to meet my Mother. There is a great friend of ours,[1] an odd-looking but high-minded woman, now in Dublin; she is a distinguished Boston doctor's wife, and a brilliant playwright. She, like so many non-Irish Americans, loves Ireland. There is a nice clever gentlemanly girl with her, Miss Beulah Dix, also of Boston. And I have sent 'em on a letter to your father, out of pure jealousy that they shall carry away the right impressions of Dublin. Say *Laus Deo* that you have no cook, or I should surely ask you to have them both to dinner when they go up to London, the week after next! because Mrs. Sutherland

[1] Mrs. Sutherland.

knows all your verses, and vastly admires you: K. T. H., likewise. I look for them at the Mitre about the 28th, so it will be a great week for me generally, with my own private emigrant thrown in.

I hope you had a nice matinée at Drury Lane. Please tell C. K. S. that his friend Mr. MacArthur is either a myth or a Perfect Terror. I posted him that Fitzgerald-Emmet humorous stuff, (which said C. K. S. was so obliging as to call, "intensely readable") in August, with a letter, in the Harpers' care; and three weeks ago, I wrote, humbly inquiring whether, &c. &c. Divil a worrud! What do you do with an editor like that? If you want a fat infant ringdove, aged six weeks, and as big as his mother, you may have mine. Our cage is a bit crowded for three. This has just struck me: that our model C. K. S. is as bad as that other gentleman,—the editor, not the bird. To wit: ask him in deep accusing tones what he ever did with the photograph (mine only and beloved print, F. H. Day *fecit*) of Millfield Lane, Hampstead Heath? Let him search his conscience for six months back. . . .

I want you to come up here before Christmas, to take pot luck in this shanty, and go on walks with me. Will you? Now that Mam is returning, you won't have undue hardship. I am going to dine with my approved Harriet Barnes tonight; she is here for some weeks. She is a painter: a beauty *and* a genius, like you. And now you'll have your hand out, with "Aoaah! G'way"! so I had best end abruptly as

Your faithful old creature, dear, (sketch)

[L. I. G.]

To Gwenllian E. F. Morgan

December, 1903.

. . . I have just had a memorial Cross put up over my dearest Aunty's grave:[1] it is Galway dark grey marble, very slender, an odd simple Celtic pattern which I adapted from an Isle of Man one! It has a rough-hewn base, and two small rough footstones. I think it exceedingly lovely. On the circle, or disc, of the Cross, I have PAX, but no other word *on* the Cross. Below it, on a tablet-like smooth surface, in front of the unpolished rock, is the inscription, which I put in Latin for the sake of brevity and the significance not possible in English. . . . The maker, Glanville of Dublin, indefatigably attentive and intelligent, as I hoped he might be. . . . Thank you, dear, for your thought of me these anniversary days, with the light upon them of the Will of God.

To Clement Shorter

1 Jan., 1904.

DEAR MR. SHORTER,—I return your good loan, thanking you with all my heart. A most Happy New Year to dear Dora and to you! Pray tell her that her puss is the joy of everybody in this house except our cat Pepper, who walks away in high dudgeon from a mi-aouing personage so extremely like himself in looks and tone. Imitation is never the sincerest flattery in the animal world, nor is it ever mistaken for it!

[1] This, in Wolvercote Cemetery, Oxford, is now the grave of L. I. G. as well.

I have something to say which you won't like, which perhaps you won't even forgive me for, though I hope you will, when you see how very honest and inevitable my reasons are. To have it out at once: I fear I can't do the Hazlitt. You will think me graceless and ungrateful. It was owing to you, I know well, that Dr. Nicoll ever heard of me, or accepted my name to stand sponsor to one of his Series books. And certainly I should have held fast to such a blessed chance five years ago, for the subject is one of the few I really know, and I have dreamed of doing a biographical Hazlitt book for almost *twenty* years! But after beating over the ground carefully, by way of preliminary, I can't see my way at all. Mr. Birrell has used all the important or useful data in Mr. Carew Hazlitt's various books; and what little original research he had put in is really excellent in its way. His tone and handling are there, of course, as everywhere else, somewhat indolent and flippant, despite his very great charm; but that should not so invalidate the book as to make a new one necessary, especially as that new one, in everything but actual criticism, would go over the same ground, and fall into inevitable comparison with its forerunner. It is, to me, a perfectly hopeless outlook. Whatever it may be to other people, this repetitive process has always been, and always will be, my bugbear. I wonder at myself for not having realised all this before: but I read Mr. Birrell too casually at first. There is nothing to add to what he has printed, except a catalogue of houses lived in, &c., and one's general impressions. Mr. Carew Hazlitt, fortunately, is very friendly to me: but what use is that under the circumstances? If it were a question of editing and annotating something of W. H., I should not hesitate; but alas! I must ask you to do me the delicate friendly service of telling Dr. Nicoll that I appreciate his offer with all gratitude; that I have tried to keep a promise —under no official seal as yet, but yet honestly given; and that I see no end to it all but for me to step out, and have the proposal cancelled that I am to be Hazlitt's biographer. Beyond the reason that I can have literally "nothing to say" in so supplementary a book, I have no other reason. But that one is only too adequate in itself. It is not the first time that I have come to the winning post when the race was over.—Please don't blame me for this exercise of my literary conscience. I am very sorry indeed over the business.

Yours to curse and ban,

L. I. GUINEY.

To the Rev. Alexander Smellie

57 S. JOHN'S ROAD, OXFORD, *Jan. 2,* 1904.

MY DEAR FRIEND,—How very kind of you to make me such a fine gift! and such a nice little gift to go with it. I rejoice to see you going forward so bravely, and using that beautiful style of yours, and I am very proud of my Smellie shelf. Many, many thanks for all; and my Mother and I wish you and dear Mrs. Smellie a year full of blessing and peace. The *Men of the Covenant* came only this morning, and you would laugh to see how industriously I have been making my preliminary skirmishes through it: for that is the sort of book I always read; and those are the times I read about. As usual, you are full of charity and relenting: I like especially the way you handle Montrose (*quem amo,* as I need not add) and you are good even to his ill King. I don't think all the years and all the documents have yet given us any historic *proof* that the latter sent the former to his fate: have they? I note how Sir Robert Moray, the best of men, gets his dues in your pages and I wonder for the thousandth time how he kept so long his affection for Lauderdale. On p. 396, isn't there a misprint at the bottom of the page *i.e.* "min*d* sweet Scotland"? That dear William Guthrie, as drawn by your namesake artist, looks exactly like a certain long-cheeked thoughtful, idiosyncratic portrait of R. L. S. at six years old: do you remember it? For R. L. S. was a true Covenanter before a French brownie got into him to make him over. Mr. Melrose puts forth most excellent work, doesn't he? I am sure all your readers must be pleased to have so large a book so light and so legible.

Ever your most grateful
L. I. GUINEY.

To Clement Shorter

10 Jan., 1904.

DEAR MR. SHORTER,—You see I have taken whole days to chew that cud. Never in all my life before have I made up my mind, unmade it, and made it up again on the first ground-plan. On the whole, I think that you are right, first, that I ought to do the book now; and next, that I can. It has taken some very hard thinking to revert to this conclusion. You are certainly a kind patient person, and a reasonable; and I thank you very much for bearing with me so gently, and standing between me and the Day of Doom: *i.e.*, Dr. Nicoll, if he knew! But let me say this: I cannot even now see my way over the obstacles I named; the fact that Mr. Birrell's *Hazlitt,* and Mr. Henley's splendid essay on Hazlitt, have come into existence while I have been loafing, as it were, in the immediate vicinity, is still a most formidable thing to a person of my temperament, so that as I say, I don't see my way through it at all. But by good luck, I see another way, round about, through underbrush, which may bring me to the end just as satisfactorily as the highroad would have done. What do you think of an interpretative biography, so to speak, which shall worry but little over outward facts, and feed itself, as it goes on, directly from Hazlitt's own intensely autobiographic pages? My one confidence is that I am a good reader; and that I may not have been in vain *his* reader ever since I was a child. I certainly know him pretty well, and love him, smooches and all. In short, if the book, by being a character-study rather than a narrative or a criticism, strictly speaking, will still fit without violence into the Series, then I shall yet undertake it. It will incur, however, the very reproach which you bestow on Mr. Birrell's work, that the quotations are too many. I can promise only this: that with me at least no one excerpt shall cover a score of pages! Everything, indeed, will depend on what encouragement you can justly give this second alternative; because you know Dr. Nicoll's scope and spirit planned for the Series, and I do not. One word more. "Strike: but hear!" I own very few of Hazlitt's books, not more than four; it would seem a common-sense move to buy the new Complete Works, or the new Works in process of completion; then it will be something of a job to give the whole heap a careful minute re-reading; lastly, there will be an immense lot of notes to take, and of extracts to copy. Nobody can do these things for me. I must work as I always do: at first-hand, and slowly. On this plan (sorry I am for it, most disconcertedly sorry!) I cannot be done, I can hardly have begun, by May. It would be the greatest imaginable boon if I might have a perfectly free hand in the matter of time. I shall not abuse it. One very serious reason for all this, which you will already have suspected, is that as I now realise I cannot afford the leisure for some four months to come. I must go on doing little miscellaneous chores, and stringing a whole rosary of future dinners, until I see plainly that I may take long weeks to do exactly what I like in, without vulgar cares. I am perfectly well, and the wheels are going; and I can make up, if all goes smoothly, for lost time during my hard 1902-3. I want to be rich enough to buy, not borrow, the books I speak of, and not to bother about earning one penny while I have the *Life* in hand. Surely, this is frank? I hope it approves itself to you also as reasonable and final. Pray tell Dora I got her most amusing and characteristic script, and give my best love both to her and Dr. Sigerson, if he be still with you. Tell him I have just opened forth my mind to Mr. Henderson, against turning Mangan into a bust in a park: I want him to be a Moral Influence, a Celtic scholarship, or some sich.

Ever yours,
L. I. GUINEY.

To Bertram Dobell

57 ST. JOHN'S ROAD, OXFORD, *2 Feb.,* 1904.

DEAR MR. DOBELL,—Your letter and the packet came together. Such a packet: an astonishing gift! I don't know whether I ought to take it, whether I am at all the right person to take it; but I do know that you are all too generous.[1] I have spent most of the afternoon over your copy, and Mr. Sayle's beautifully written one, and my opinion of Alabaster goes up and up. There are really a score of splendid sonnets among them to go into an English treasury, and he is quite worthy of the services of the University Press, and of a more learned editor. The editing, however, takes on great future attraction; when I get to him, I daresay I shall find further clues in the Bodleian, as he must have been very well known indeed. Over against that day, I make but one stipulation: and that

[1] Mr. Dobell gave L. I. G. all the material he had collected about William Alabaster (1577-1640), with full rights to use it in the edition of that poet which she projected.

is that the whole story of these MSS. and of how I came to be the very proud and somewhat abashed possessor of them, shall be set down for the benefit of Elia's pet, Antiquity. Some day I must see both originals. And I shall have no end of comments and questions to bring forth. Am I to keep this odd volume of Dr. Drake's? Prof. Littledale's letter is most suggestive. Though I know I cannot attend to the work for a year, or nearly a year, yet I shall shortly ask Mr. Hart, the Controller of the Press here, what he thinks about publishing Alabaster; and you shall hear of any progress in that direction. For the rest, any "thank you," like Macbeth's "Amen," "sticks i' the throat." I can never thank you or repay you; so I go bankrupt with joy. I hope I may live to see you quite satisfied with my handling of your noble poet, my temporary fellow Papist.

Most gratefully and ever faithfully yours,

L. I. GUINEY.

Do you suppose Mr. Sayle's St. John's Coll. original is in Alabaster's own hand? He was fifty, I find, in 1627, the date which it bears. If he wrote the poems then, *he was a Catholic for the second time.* This rotary motion was common in the early seventeenth century! I disagree with you already . . . about sonnets I-XXII not being by the same hand as the rest; nor do I think them much inferior, though of less scope. III, XII, XVII, XXVIII and XX are beautiful, surely.

L. I. G.

To Bertram Dobell

57 S. John's Road, Oxford, *Feb. 2,* 1904.

Dear Mr. Dobell,—You will like to see this. What authority Mr. Hazlitt had for printing without qualification that "W. A." is Alabaster, I know not. It is likely enough, of course. Another possible guess would be William Austin. I am having the pieces copied, and should like you to look them over some day. No sonnets there, apparently. Fr. Hungerford Pollen, of the Farm St. Jesuit Church, has given me a lot of most valuable referenda to original MSS. at the Record Office, Stonyhurst Coll., etc., which I hope, later, to follow up. Did you know that Alabaster started to be a Jesuit? He seems to have lost and drowned his beautiful poetic gift in running after cabalistic philosophy, as so many did in that troubled age. This is all for today, except best wishes ever from

Yours,
L. I. G.

To Bertram Dobell

57 S. John's Road, Oxford, *16 March,* [1904.]

Dear Mr. Dobell,—Another nice gift! Thank you so much for the poems. Do you suppose I would give away, on the appearance of a finer copy, a book whose flyleaf bore such a pleasant inscription? I note the new numbers, and like them all. Who is the Balladist Parson? the Rev. J. Woodfall Ebbsworth of the Roxburghe Ballads? I like *him* chiefly because he likes Charles II.

Aren't you quite a prolific writer this month of March, A. D. 1904?

Perhaps I can get out of printing Alabaster in Latin. It is great fun to be able to read Mr. Bullen's D. N. B. article, and see at how many points he is wrong. I tell you, it is rare sport to know more about even the outside of any old poets than Mr. Bullen does! and that chaste pleasure is not likely to fall in one's way more than once in a lifetime. Thirty pounds seems to me a fortune. I hardly suppose anybody would give me that. However, I shall make the venture by next Christmas or so.

I shall get B. & F.[1] off to you tomorrow. It is like packing a Hippopotamus.

Yours faithfully,
L. I. GUINEY.

To Bertram Dobell

OXFORD, *Apr. 16,* 1904.

DEAR MR. DOBELL,—You will think me (or at least you ought to think me,) a Hungrateful Ussy. I have been horribly busy, and not very well, and feel yet as if I had the Andes and the Alps to stagger along under, though the ponderosity is only a cold. Of course I am immensely grateful to you (how could I possibly be otherwise?) for your interest and genial kindness. I have little doubt that the sort of editing Mr. E. V. Lucas might propose to me would be the sort of editing I can do, and should love to do. My only worry is my present but very non-habitual behindhandedness! and until I can

[1] The 1679 folio of Beaumont and Fletcher, which she was selling to Mr. Dobell.

clear away three promised longish magazine articles and two shortish books, I have hardly a right to my salt. I shan't go on selling books, nor need to, once I have caught up with arrears; and can then pay scot as I go. The Hazlitt work I haven't touched at all yet, but must do it this summer. Although my head is always running more or less on W. H., I mean to read him all through again *en bloc,* before I begin; and that will be, I think, a day of woe for you! for I shall delight as much in borrowing as you do in lending.

My little *Emmet* [1] is but an intermezzo: such as it is, I should of course like to hear how well you can manage to like it, or in what point it falls flat, according to one of the gentlest readers it is likely to get. Thank you very much for letting me see the enclosed notices. They are joyous and just. I feel, with you, that friends' commendations have too *à priori* a flavour to stand in one's mind at their real value. Why friends of poets, or owners of race-horses, or mothers of babies, should not be, on principle, unbiassed judges, has always rather beaten me!

All things good to you, including some playtime before the most captivating month in the year is de-Apriled. I haven't had a "day off" for many weeks, but shall take to the road or the river soon, I hope. (I go alone, with sixpence and a stick, or an extra length of rope in the canoe; and come home by starlight feeling like the Great Mogul.)

Your ever obliged and faithful
L. I. GUINEY.

---

[1] *Robert Emmet* . . . by L. I. G. David Nutt, London, 1904.

To Clement Shorter

57 S. John's Road, Oxford, *16 Apr.*, 1904.

Dear Mr. Shorter,—I have an accumulation of Thank Yous to tie to your door, like a May-basket: for the Historical Exhibition ticket; for the reviews you kindly sent me; for the reminder I hardly need, that it is a very long time indeed since I last saw a certain enchanting Library, and the fair Missus and the Master thereof; for the *Tatler*, with the heady praises of *Emmet*, and for all your friendly and urgent remarks on the subject of Dr. Nicoll's *Hazlitt*. The keynote of that Series has been struck twice with something like arresting power and beauty; and I am thankful that I shall be at a measurable distance from the *Arnold* and particularly from the *Newman!* My own keenly-felt but innocent delays preclude me from saying much more than that I shall do my best when I can, and as quickly as ever I can. I mean to read over W. H. *en bloc* again for a fresh final impression, but I am not sure yet that I can read him in the dress of a new Complete Edition, despite the splendid Introduction by Henley, and all the pictures and notes! However, I dare say I shall end by abjectly borrowing the whole set from you. I want a quiet four or five weeks in sea-air, and the thing shall be done, for good or ill. Once I get out of this moil and wreck of arrears, I shall not be a prize procrastinate a second time. It plagues me now beyond words.

I was immensely interested in Prof. Saintsbury's programme, and have heard from him directly. His plan, being extra-lyrical, is a larger one altogether than my cherished notion of nearly *a score* of years, which it may even do away with. But I am so turrible fond of them Carolians, that it delights me to see them summoned up by better wands than mine. There are three or four, not named in the prospectus, well worth inclusion. I say ever:

"Beati Swashbuckler, orate pro nobis—"

With constant love to Dora (whom Prof. York Powell was commending in italics and capitals when I saw him last,—he is mending fast now,—)

Yours as ever,
L. I. GUINEY.

To Bertram Dobell

OXFORD, *August 9*, 1904.

DEAR MR. DOBELL,—Only yesterday I was thinking hard of you, wondering how you were, etc., so it is doubly pleasant to have your script and parcel today. The little book I had never seen. I agree with you that *Flavia* and *Home-Travell* are charming, but I have no least notion of their authorship. The variations in Donne's Valediction (from the accepted version, I mean,) are interesting, despite misprints. Also, I am glad to learn that Alabaster's epigram appeared in print as early as 1658. There are at least two 16th cent. MS. copies of it here in Oxford. When W. A. drew up his little autobiography in a half-dozen paragraphs for the English College books at Rome, he mentioned *"quidam Reynaldus"* as a cause, or the cause, of his conversion;

and Foley's *Records of the English Province of the Society of Jesus* (a most valuable work) actually queries Reynaldus as "Cardinal Pole."

I have read every word of the criticisms, and of your most reasonable replies; but, do you know, I wish you hadn't broken into the part-song at all. My view, no doubt, is an extreme one; but I think it a sort of crime against the craft to care a farthing what they say. Hang 'em all, and write for antiquity, like Lamb, if you can. *Litera scripta manet,* if it has the seed in it; and if it hasn't, why should the sower fret who has done his best and lived his hour? Whatever is not "right," in the Ruskinian sense, will spoil beautifully, all by itself. Certainly no poet should break his peace, even to help it spoil. To print is human, but to growl at home divine.

Thank you immensely for liking *Patrins*. I took it up last week, after forgetting all about it for years, and it struck me as a terribly knobby, breathless, young book: much younger than it should be, by the calendar. There's no coherence to it. You might say that the writer's heart was in the right place, and that there's a lot of literary idealism; but there one ends. I really don't quite make out as yet what I am for; but I suspect you will never see shore if you look for truly mellowed work, with wholeness of aim and effect, from me. I haven't purpose enough to steer a bee across a dust-bin, such as might lie between him and the rose-beds in the garden. "To travel is a better thing than to arrive": that's my device. But the man who said that had the genius which couldn't help arriving too.

I return all the precious lendings, and I am most

thankful to you. We are as usual here. My Mother goes Oct. 1, unless I can bewitch her to stay, by means of some undiscovered potion. I am very busy at present with proofs of my chaotic *Memoir of Hurrell Froude.* The Methuens wouldn't let me have slip-proofs, and I couldn't help making a mess of page-proofs: so there'll be the piper to pay, on my luckless part.

Do you know Thomas Stanley?[1] I must send you my little edition (Tutin) when it comes out. He is a crystal, is Stanley. Be as kind as ever you can to my friend, Mr. Dobell, won't you? I am sure it is worth while.

Faithfully yours,
L. I. GUINEY.

To Clement Shorter

20 FARNDON ROAD, OXFORD, *Nov. 24,* 1904.

DEAR MR. SHORTER,—Thank you so much for your nice article, and the compliment imbedded in it. But I wonder where you detected the note of revolt in that poem, or any of mine? Wherever they are to be construed as even remotely autobiographic, I thought they had absolutely no bone to pick with Fate! You are a keen critic, but I fancy I have you there. I have moved, my Mother having returned to "Yankland" (H. Froude's disrespectful word), and am most comfortably domiciled here, with all my belongings, in a conjoint housekeeping with my friend Miss Harriet Anderson. If I could see you and Dora occasionally, I should begin even to feel intelligent again. My love to her. She

[1] *Thomas Stanley* (1625-1678), edited by L. I. G. Tutin, Hull, 1907.

will like this frantically picturesque snow, if you have it adorning St. John's Wood.

Yours ever gratefully,
L. I. GUINEY.

To Florence Warren

1904.

. . . Thank you for liking Orinda: nice old girl, Orinda.[1] . . . The only other one of mine in the series will be a Wither. But I have done, with delight, a thorough edition of the lyrics of that almost perfect lyrist Thomas Stanley. This will be out in the Autumn. My big long-delayed Froude[2] appears then, too. I rather dread being found out in Oxford for a literary fellow! Anonymity is like a rose-water bath to me. . . .

Mr. [William Dean] Howells, and Mildred (lovely as ever), were at the Encaenia for his D. C. L., or is it LL.D.? and after. . . . I miss my poor York Powell,[3] of whom I saw a great deal, at his own request, during his last illness. . . . He was my oldest Oxford friend, the one I could talk with most freely. He told the Bradleys that he "loved little Guiney," and he wrote me, when he saw my small Emmet book: "You're an historian." I don't often treasure up compliments; but I shall like to keep these. . . .

Thanks many and heartfelt for all your goodness

[1] *Katherine Philips, the Matchless Orinda* (1631-1664). Selected Poems, edited by L. I. G. J. R. Tutin, Hull, 1904.
[2] *Hurrell Froude* (1803-1836), edited by L. I. G. Methuen, 1904.
[3] Frederick York Powell, Regius Professor of Modern History at Oxford, died 8th May, 1904.

about the flowers: one of the strongest invisible links between you and your

L. I. G.

To Dora Sigerson

20 FARNDON ROAD, OXFORD, *27 Apr.*, 1905.

DEAREST DORA,—If you're in town, do you want to look up a very dear friend of mine, in the person of Dr. C. N. Greenough (pronounced in the American fashion "Green-o") who is at 29 Queen Square, W. C.? I thought I would write to you instead of arming him with a formal letter. He would enormously enjoy meeting C. K. S. and you. Your lord may know his name, as he is joint author with his friend Prof. Barrett Wendell of a standard text-book on Literature. "Dr." Greenough is not M.D., but Ph.D., and Tutor of Harvard University. He is really a splendid fellow to the marrow of him, a real lover of letters, and of animals and of all things of good report, and Harriet Anderson, my housemate here, and myself, always say he is *the* best company out of doors, and something very like the best indoors. He is just a bit shy; but don't take that for formality, of which he has none. He stayed many months here at the Bodleian, and about three weeks ago betook himself to the Br. Museum. He has some acquaintanceship in London with Mr. Gosse and other literary folk; but I want him to know you: and you are sure, I think, to like him. So I commend dear old "Dooley" (as we call him for fun) to your benignity.

I wish, by the way, that you would both run in to see

me some day this spring, especially if you'll tell me so on a postcard the day before: for now I am in "a house, not a hut"—the phrase is my Mother's,—and you won't have sour cake and a withered beldam to serve it! Please appear, Dora! Also, I should be so grateful if you'd tell me about Hester and the baby, how he gets on, what they have named him, &c. (I hope he is just Sigerson Piatt.) I am rather fagged at present. I find more than enough to do; but it isn't "litthrachoor." Love to C. K. S., and commend me to birds and beasts as their mistress's constant old friend and admirer,

LOUISE I. GUINEY.

To Dora Sigerson

20 FARNDON ROAD, OXFORD, *18 July,* [1905].

DEAREST DORA,—Thanks for your sweet note. Yes, I am well, and happy enough, too, but terribly drowsy of soul and brain. I often wonder if I am going to change into something else, like Daphne and Arethusa and the other fabled wenches! Whether it is sleepy Oxford, or mine own increasing age, I wot not. But I am literary no more: no, not for a day: and never would know a trochee from a lozenge, as a Boston wag once said. I wish you could spend a day here with us before we leave the pretty garden and go bag and baggage (about August 25) to 6, Winchester Road. The latter is an unfurnished house which my mate Harriet Anderson has just signed a lease for; and she is going to New York to fetch back her own stored furniture. This house is much the nicer: not an 'ole like the one I got along in when I was all alone. If you'd come up *over* some Sunday, you and the Man, I should like it well. Your new book seems to be getting hearty reviews. Good luck to it!

I saw Harry and Katharine Hinkson for ten minutes, when they passed through Oxford with the Whitefriars Club, about a month ago: a rotund pair. Kind as ever. I wish you'd tell me any news, or some news, of one Dr. Sigerson, and of the Piatt baby, whose name I don't even know; and where your new house is (Bucks?) and —whether you have found peace, as the Salvation folk are so fond of saying, and—hevery-think. I haven't any summer plans. I wanted to go back to Yorkshire, where there's such air to breathe, with two of my two-score lately-arrived American friends: but I wasn't rich enough, so continued to vegetate, and compose myself, and abide.

How are all the dear beasties? We have one amusing and ironic small dog. Mrs. Moulton writes as usual that she is BLUE and ILL, but will hold court on Fridays. She hasn't the remotest conception of what melancholy and ill-health really are: she's the *ennuyé imaginaire*. This coolness is lovely. I die in the heat; don't you? It enrages me particularly in England, being a mean plagiarism. Love to you, and *addio*. Don't forget quite your mute but not unfaithful old friend,

L. I. G.

To George Norton Northrop

OXFORD, *Oct. 2*, 1905.

YOU DEAR FELLOW,—It is such a "right" poem! Thank you for it. You know that it is clearly our mission, the mission of us Americans in England, to beat down (by what we are and believe, not by what we say) the too callous spirit of caste and custom which has come upon the Old World. It takes patience and delicacy to stand effectively against it, while you are, so to speak, a guest. It cannot be doubted that we have very much to learn here; but just as surely, we have that one thing to sow and teach. Don't get homesick! You will find plenty to interest you, in another fortnight. Meanwhile, may this granny take you on a walk? I shall be lunching at 187 Woodstock Road (Heaven send that I have the number right, and that it isn't 167 or 189!) on Friday; and if you will call there at 2.30 P.M., I will take you on a nice ramble of say eight or nine miles, through places where you may not have been, and which are good to look at. . . .

Cheer up, Little Brother!

Yours faithfully,
L. I. Guiney.

To George Norton Northrop

Oct. 31st, 1905.

Dear Poet,—You may have noticed my befogged condition shay voo? I have passed most of my time in bed, barking, ever since; or I should have thanked you before for your friendly offices in giving me a chance to meet Prof. Raleigh. He is exactly like his work, simple and fearless and thorough, and with wonderful sensitiveness of appreciation. I loved him none the less that his Look is so like R. L. S.! Altogether, he sent me on my way rejoicing, as Dons do not invariably do. Isn't it a glorious joke, his really being here to leaven Oxford? . . .

Yours as ever,
L. I. G.

To E. W. B. Nicholson [1]

6 Winchester Road, Oxford, *Nov. 28,* 1905.

Dear Mr. Nicholson,—I think I am not mistaken in recognizing your handwriting (I don't see how you manage to work it so hard, and keep it so firm and beautiful too!) on the envelope of *Pro Bodleio* [2] which has newly reached me. If so, may I not send in person my very warm thanks? I wished vehemently for another copy; I said so to Mr. Doble; and I suppose that "unweariedest spirit in doing courtesies" must have told you in turn. The result much delights me. I wish Convocation would vote to you a grant of immortality, the whole of it to be spent *in loco!*

You will have taken interest, I know, in the October *Century,* with its two (?) new portraits of Shelley. I appear to be the only person who labours under the

[1] Edward Williams Byron Nicholson, Bodley's Librarian from 1882 until his death in 1912, was a man of singularly interesting personality. His chief work, the reorganization of the Bodleian Library, carried out despite infinite obstacles, is a sufficient and lasting monument to his talents, though he was distinguished in Celtic and other research. His advanced views, together with an uncompromising manner, gained him considerable opposition from folk who could not truly estimate his single-minded devotion to Bodley and scholarship and the justice, vigour and depth of his character: those who could, however, found him a stimulating ever-courteous friend, and sympathized whole-heartedly with his aims.

[2] A spirited and amusing protest, in pamphlet form, against an attempt to desecrate the Proscholium, Boldey's "vaulted walke," by using it as a bicycle-shed. The attempt failed.

obsession that the first portrait, the unfinished pencil sketch, is really Leigh Hunt. I am having an animated discussion on the subject, illustrated, with my old friend the Editor, Mr. Richard Watson Gilder. The whole matter could be settled, I fancy, in the Hope Collection.

With every best wish,

Very sincerely yours,

L. I. GUINEY.

To Gwenllian E. F. Morgan

[1905].

. . . I have two books I am crazy to lend you. . . . One is a most noble and remarkable seventeenth-century love-story of "the warres," called *Blount of Breckenhow,* written by Beulah Dix, an American girl I know. It is all in the form of make-believe letters, done with a very sure and lightly archaic hand, and at fault in very few particulars, being based on genuine historic knowledge. Macmillan has the book. I mean to praise and commend it on all sides. In general, I despise so-called "historic fiction," but this is a magnificent little work, and I went through it prancing.

To Mary Winefride Day

6 WINCHESTER ROAD, OXFORD, *Feb. 16,* 1906.

DEAR,—I dropped the *Weekly* in the mud this morning, and disqualified it so that I am only cutting out the Oxford news for you. How do you get on in the "bluidie Warres"? Fr. Henry Day was here yesterday. Not the least part of his niceness is his unmistakable looking like you. We all got laughing very much over an anecdote of the Rector's. You know he was at Wroxton a fortnight ago. Lord North had some awful bores to tea, stood them out awhile, and then peacefully went to sleep in his chair. Butler, at the end of twenty minutes, in his ear: "Please, my Lord, Mr. and Mrs. Thing are going!" His Lordship, still half-dozing, but gloriously candid: "*Thank God for that!*"

Harriet, and I, and pretty much everybody, have been writing little articles for that forthcoming Calendar. Fr. McNabb, O. P., the Prior of Woodchester, lectures in our box of a drawing-room on the 26th. The weather is but so-so. I hope you get the sun down there? Don't mind writing till you are out of chaos. Much love to you from,

L. I. G.

To Wilfrid Meynell

6 WINCHESTER ROAD, OXFORD, *5 March,* 1906.

DEAR MR. MEYNELL,—My friend and housemate, Miss Harriet Anderson of New York whom you (luckless man!) do not know, wishes me, whom you do know, to write to you on a subject which is very interesting to us at present. We have been casting about, since we settled down together in Oxford, to see what we could do to increase community of feeling among local Catholics, further intelligent interest in Catholic ideals, and get a rather centrifugal congregation together, not indeed in a socialistic way, but in a human way. Every unit can help at that! So, for one thing, we have started some evening Lectures (the credit is my colleague's and not mine) in our own drawing-room, on Catholic questions of the hour. (Said drawing-room is a tiny box; with all the ordinary furniture out, and hired chairs in, placed a-row, we can get but forty into it as a maximum. Next year, the scene of battle will be a fine large ground-floor studio, hard by.) They have been immensely successful. We invite Oxford Papists in relays, of all sorts and classes, discourage evening dress, encourage discussion, and serve coffee and biscuits. Fr. Hugh Benson began the series of Lectures in December, coming down specially from Cambridge: his subject was The Conversion of England: a masterly paper. Next, in January, came Fr. Joseph Rickaby, on The Origin of Universities; and last month we had the Prior of Woodchester, Fr. McNabb, O. P., on Liberal Catholicism. (I think you know that quicksilver genius?) This month, being Lenten, has no nominee at all; but Mr. Urquhart comes in May, Fr. Bede Camm, O. S. B., in June, and we want

YOU

for April. Can you manage that? and will you? If you will talk about any subject of current, or lasting, Catholic interest, we should be enormously grateful; nor need you prepare a new paper if you prefer to furbish up an old one. All will be new and welcome to our audience; and you have many admirers among them already. Now pray don't refuse, busy *ad unguis* as we know you to be. This would be our programme, if only you would ratify it. Apr. 28, Saturday, Mr. and Mrs.

Meynell leave Paddington for Oxford. Apr. 29, H. A. and L. I. G. give a little modest At Home, chiefly that literary undergrads may gaze upon Mrs. Meynell: then off we all go to Benediction, in order to show you both how bad a choir we have at St. Aloysius'! Lastly, on the 30th, your Lecture; and when it is all over, a late supper as usual on these occasions: this one as delectable as wits and goodwill can devise, to which should be bidden the two resident Catholic dons of Oxford, both very good, and both very clever. A happy week-end, it would be, for Miss Anderson and me!

Oxford Catholics are a rather provincial set, but they are appreciative. (Mrs. Meynell will spot this for a contradiction in terms!) Our Rector, Fr. Arthur Day, S. J., much approves of our small enterprise; and the whole Presbytery usually turns up on Lecture nights. We looked quite festive, a fortnight ago, with two Dominicans and two Benedictines in full regalia! besides the Jesuit Fathers and the miscellaneous faithful.

When you come (I won't be so cruel to our hopes as to say "if") will you not let Miss Anderson, after the American fashion, send you the two return railway tickets? You see this is a long notice ahead, in order that you may have time and opportunity to be kind to us, and arrange to come as our guests. I send this to the *Tablet* office, because though I know you have left that dear Palace Court house, I lack the new address. My love, and my salutations *empressées* to the queen poet. Tell her the pudding will be spoiled unless she is here.

Yours very faithfully,

L. I. Guiney.

To Mary Winefride Day

BOSTON: CORPUS CHRISTI, *June 14,* 1906.

Mary Winefride ever dear, your blessed letter is here. On leaving Oxford at thirty hours' notice I bequeathed all my mail to an old (non-Catholic American) friend living there, to open, inquire into, answer and forward. As it happened, I had had a rather special thought of a few, you among them; and I asked another friend, Mrs. Bolton, to write to you for me, as I have no doubt she did. I was going to introduce her and her two adorable boys to you when you came to us. She is an exquisite character, brave, sweet, and cheery, and has seen much trouble; she is a near neighbour of ours, and you would like her well for her strong understanding affection for one A. F. D., S. J., now happily reigning: whom God preserve! Well, I no sooner got home from Evian [1] (very fagged too, quite as fagged as I went) than I was cabled for, with the alarming news that my Mother was very ill. You can imagine my anxiety, unrelieved until I arrived here. She was immensely better then: that was three days ago. And now I tell her she is "well." For she can sit up a whole afternoon, and read. She is weak, indeed, too tender, as it were, to be dressed, or even carried out into the air. But on the mend she certainly is, *laus Deo*. I am a goodish sort of nurse, and very glad to be here. As for England and the laburnums, I simply mustn't think of them at present, or I should whimper. I think Mother and I will get out of town together before long. I am so glad you are

[1] Evian-les-Bains, France.

settled at last. I hope the crippled garden is recovering, and affording you some comfort. Nearness to a town is indeed what one misses, except when off on a gypsy trail across country, "wifeless, roofless, flagonless, alone," as I like to be now and then. (I have never known anything else in petticoats which enjoys being alone. But there were anchoresses once, if not hermitresses!) The goldenest of good luck to you, Châtelaine! It shall be as you say about the *Catholic World*. But you haven't the least idea what pleasure I used to take in doing up that little weekly parcel with your name on it. I send our Magazine to five addresses. Do you get that every month?

Now about your Brother (Harriet often alludes to him as "*our* Brother," by the way. You know he has stood so splendidly by her lecture scheme, month after month; he always comes, and always makes a speech; and he stays to supper with us; and makes us proud as peacocks thereby). I quite agree with you about him, that he should have stayed longer at Lynton. We mustn't let that bright sword wear its scabbard too thin. He is most certainly not as harassed and tired out as he was this time a year ago; but he needs rest now, in a way, almost as much as then. He ought to have it, a month or six weeks of it, straight away. Everything will be quiet at Oxford, and I should suppose he, even he, could take a furlough without scruple! I will tell you that I have been advising him very strongly, only just now, to take a sea-voyage, on the slow boats of the Atlantic Transport (London and New York) or preferably, the Leyland Line (Liverpool and Boston) to an

American port; but not to stay too long ashore, because our noisy cities in the summer heats are most exhausting. The one thing the matter with him is just "nerves": and that is never understood properly, never prescribed for properly, never even sympathised with properly, in England. And yet it is more terrible, if not checked, than almost any form of disease, and completely cancels one's energy and usefulness. Only it *can* always be checked, thank the Lord. It always makes for the best people, the crystals of the human race. If you agree with me, I do wish you would urge the sea-voyage. Perhaps he will mention it when he writes to you. You two are wonderfully alike, in some ways. Your kind of sensitiveness, and your kind of courage, are exactly the same: I "remove" my hat to them as the finest things I know. I wish you could put to sea with him, and take care of him on shore, for the time being. You know I never held forth about his health before! though I have always had an eye—may I call it a sisterly eye?—upon it. No wonder your little Lynton nuns liked him. If I knew absolutely nothing about him, I should love him for his mien at the Altar. It ought to attract instantly everybody who cares for Our Master and His business.

Well, hereby endeth, etc. You will have my provisional address from Miss Crocker. Harriet will beguile her widowed state by going to France for July and August. Salutations from yours ever affectionately,

L. I. G.

P. S. Just as I finished, in came Fr. Gasson, S. J., Professor of Philosophy at Boston College, a great friend of my Mother's. Almost the first thing he said to me was (he is English by birth himself) "Why don't you get some of the English Jesuits over here to pay us a call? There's too little intercourse. Your Rector, Fr. Day—tell him to come here, and I'll look after him well, and show him our great Novitiate at Woodstock." Wasn't that odd? But you see Mother had been telling him of our Oxford Church.

To George Norton Northrop

302 Beacon St., Boston, *20 July,* 1906.

My dear Poet,—This is but to tell you how glad I was to hear from you. I had been thinking of you, in part because I lately met Mr. [Arthur] Upson. (I have dined out just once, and there was he at my good ear! A sensitive lovable chap, I think, with right stuff in him.) Of course you'd appreciate my beloved Yorkshire: mine by predilection, and yours by pedigree. I never saw you to tell you that I browsed a good part of the day in the Bodleian after Northrops: enough to satisfy me that the only proper way to trace them intelligently is 1st, to connect with the local (county) Archaeological Society; 2nd, to visit the villages named, and search the Registers. I fancy we're a homesick pair, you and I! Keep in touch with me until September, at any rate; for as like as not, I shall be going back to Oxford with you, just before the Michaelmas Term begins. Which do you notice most on our native soil—the noises, or the twang? As for my chief and lifelong enemy, the summer heats (in an accursed merciless mood at present), I have to gaze steadfastly at peach-crates, clam-shells, or "some such whatever," in order to clutch at the fact that there is a law of compensation.

Meanwhile, things are not cheery *chez nous*. I had my Mother at Plymouth for a fortnight, under the eye of a friend we both love; and she was able to get up and dress every morning early, walk a little in the woods, take automobile drives, and so on. But since we came back to town, she has been terribly weak and feverish. I have not been out, for more than ten minutes a day, for a week, and have stayed up for these last two nights. I have a good Dr., but must now get a nurse too. The outlook is a very anxious one. Do you happen to remember our clever fat impossible young choir master Mr. B, who walked with us, a year ago, to Sutton Courtney? He turned up here yesterday, on his way to Cincinnati, where his professional lot has been cast. His un-English "push" will serve him there, belike.

This morning brought a long delayed letter from Harriet. She will be at Niers-les-Bains until October. Philla Fletcher has been my faithfullest news-agent, in that drowsy town of both our loves. Well, God be wi' ye! I wish you had carried off the Newdigate. Have a happy summer.

Yours ever,
L. I. GUINEY.

To Bertram Dobell

6 WINCHESTER RD., OXFORD, *Feb. 7,* 1907.

DEAR MR. DOBELL,—Thank you so much for the precious loan. Polsted is a satiric wag, don't you think?

I mean to find out something about him. Might I lend the book to Miss Morgan for a few days, of course by registered post? She is the carefullest person. You were so good to send me Dr. Brown's beautiful article. Luckily, I know it; it was one of the very first things I ever read about H. V. This I will return with *The Exciseman*. It is delightful—this news of Mr. Bullen's editorship. *Floreant!* he and his ancient and honourable concern. If I didn't keep a pretty sharp eye upon L. I. G., she would do at every turn, day after day, just such crazy things as addressing "Charing Cross Road, Oxford"! I always think it so cheap a matter to get up a reputation for eccentricity: and devoutly intend to "be as great a humdrum as I can," as Hurrell Froude used to say.

Best wishes from your grateful

L. I. GUINEY.

To Bertram Dobell

6 WINCHESTER ROAD, OXFORD, *Feb. 14,* [1907.]

DEAR MR. DOBELL,—I return this with a thousand thanks. Very interesting I found it, and so did Miss Morgan. In her letter lately received, she says: "I quite agree with your view that the whole thing is a Satire. There are two points which show that Ezekiel knew something of Breconshire: on p. 23 is a reference to Humphrey Bamster, a decidedly Brecon touch, and on p. 56, a quotation from James Howell's Letters. I know nothing of the name Polsted hereabouts: nor anywhere, for the matter of that." And again: "Pp. 95

and 104, 'our poet,' 'the poet,' etc. How tantalizing! Why could he not give names? Both verses excessively Vaughanish: like unpublished poems of our dear twins."

I ran the name Polsted to earth, in the Bodleian, in Hasted's Kent, in Berry's Sussex, in Rawl. MS. B. 429, and in the London Visitation of 1633. In all is a Henry Polsted of London, Merchant, who is also of Stoneham, Sussex and of Losely, Surrey: the Lon. Vis. *only* names among his sons an "Ezekell." He was born, apparently, between 1623 and 1630. I have no doubt this is our man, but must trace him further. Perhaps his marriage connected him with Breconshire. I am full of curiosity about the *Cambria Triumphans,* and wish myself at the Br. Museum this moment, to see it. Some future day I shall probably make bold to borrow this *Exciseman* of you again. Keep well! and believe me ever most gratefully yours,

L. I. GUINEY.

Thank you so much, too, for the Cowley-Alabaster hint. Likely enough, surely. "Worshipful" is a somewhat odd adjective for Dr. W. A., but just the word a boy would like to use. I have never seen the original edition of *Poetical Blossoms,* and should be delighted to do so, as I am rather desperately fond of Abraham Couleius, *decus, deliciae aevi sui,* as his Abbey monument calls him. What publisher would like to do a nice reprint of Habington and of Quarles, do you think? The two dear fellows are being overlooked by everybody, and deserve it not.

L. I. G.

To Gwenllian E. F. Morgan

[1907.]

. . . I enjoy the almost daily society of Mr. and Mrs. Wilfred Wilberforce. . . . He is a priceless creature, all love and wit and justness, like his own father, Newman's dear Henry W. He is getting old: it breaks my heart to have such people age and die in this piggish world. The only comfort is Carlyle's memorable phrase: "The Heavens stint not their bounty; they send us generous hearts into every generation."

(I wonder if you have ever had my silly sense of personal permanence? I feel like a spectator in a city balcony, seeing the long procession pass, banners and drums and all. That I am really in it with the rest is a comic, an incredible notion!)

This is the loveliest little edition of *Saint Paul!* I worship that poem these many years now (you first introduced me), and know much of it by heart. . . . I have bought and distributed in my day, several copies of the red cloth-covered edition with the black cross. Hardly anybody seems to know what a magnificent thing is this output of Mr. Myers' youth. . . .

To Clement Shorter

6 Winchester Rd., Oxford, *16 March,* 1907.

Dear Mr. Shorter,—Thank you so much for your kind note, and for the cutting. I am troubled about mention of the *Hazlitt.* Was it not understood by Dr. Nicoll (who, after all, never has personally broached the subject to me) that extremely grateful as I was and shall always be to him and to you for reposing that much confidence in my abilities, I saw clearly, on second thought, that I could not take up the work? The fact that, if one could judge by journalistic comment when the announcement was made, the book clearly was not wanted, after Mr. Birrell's, would not weigh much with me who had dreamed of doing a book about W. H. (for full twenty years!) except that, frankly, I lack courage to go on with anything new or considerable. It is simply impossible. Whatever fire was originally in me has died out for lack of a flue; I am, I will not say embittered—my worst enemy would allow that I have no grievances!—but atrophied. If I ever finish long-begun and long-interrupted tasks like the Vaughan, Alabaster, St. Frideswide, &c. I shall do almost more than now I hope for; but I shall never be able to plan and carry out with my old zest. You don't know what it is to have to live on public praise; to have done your very best in composing or editing some sixteen books, and to draw from them in the lump, thanks to one unhallowed cause or another, not three guineas a year, seldom as much as forty-five shillings! I have never been a particularly prolific producer of prose, most certainly a very sparse one of verse; yet I hardly ever get anything printed at home without immense preliminary trouble, and repeated suings to this Magazine and that: living meanwhile on smiles and compliments, and no shekels. And here in England nobody but you, apparently, will print me at all! I have taken the trouble to put pride in my pocket, and try the *Spectator*, for instance, repeatedly, since 1901: quite in vain. You recommended the *Westminster* for that essay-let, the other day: of course I failed there too. You must see that all your most friendly championing of mediæval unpopular me is, in Dante's fit phase, "foam in water, and smoke in air." I am a rounded and perfect Failure, so far as getting on in this world is concerned. And therefore, knowing that, though I keep up a brisk step, and a grin, I have no least heart to undertake Hazlitt, or anything else which is a fresh enterprise. Mark you, I have never uttered a literary jeremiad in any other ear. Remembrance of all your persistent kindness has, so to speak, forced it out of me. I want you to see how inevitable and unalterable is my conviction on the subject; I want you to realise that I am incapable of acting upon mere whim, especially where the wishes are concerned of so good a friend as you have always been to me. So that is the long and short of it: don't ask me into jousts, for all my lances are broken. I am writing to Dora. Congratulations on your Doctorate!

Yours always,
L. I. GUINEY.

To Clement Shorter

6 WINCHESTER ROAD, OXFORD, *20 March,* [1907.]

DEAR MR. SHORTER,—My warm thanks for your commonsense and most friendly letter. I agree with every word of it, though that doesn't mend matters. I didn't, however, mean in the least that I was waiting for a personal communication from Dr. Nicoll: goodness, no! not I. But what I did mean was that perhaps he would not feel my defection so much as if the idea of getting me to do the work had been his, and not yours, in the beginning. I think you will have to believe me quite literally when I say that it is not perversity which drives me to write of "seventeenth-century poets, and people who are not of the slightest interest to this generation." I have to write of what I know best, and I have never learned to run with the crowd. Nor do I belong at all, I fear, to this generation: that I do not has been a lifelong worry to me, and no source of silly pride. As for Hazlitt, I did write about him, too, before there was any Hazlitt revival: I do not consider now that I know enough to set up as an authority on Hazlitt, or even step into any field where Mr. Birrell has gleaned, least of all show up in a series enriched with such magnificent work as Dr. Barry's *Newman*. You say three weeks would do it. But you don't know my slow ways. Three months wouldn't do it: and though £100 is a pleasant sum to earn, what would keep me afloat while I was making for the £100? You must forgive me for being dead against my own handling of what I own to be a most attractive subject. It would only be pulled to pieces, that book, and Dr. Nicoll growled at for including it; and though I once had an excellent faculty to stomach hostile criticism, I cannot face it now.

Don't say I have "vast knowledge." I have only vast appreciation, and a fair, not a phenomenal, memory. My one distinction, *i. e.*, my curse, is that I am driven to do what I have done and do, in letters, and cannot make a rational and business-like choice of subjects as many people can, to the augmenting of their reputation, purse, and general content. I am a bad wry-necked sort altogether, and you would do well to wash your hands of me. *Sum quod sum.* I have it in me yet to make an admirable proof-reader for somebody who can make a satisfactory *Hazlitt* for Dr. Nicoll: but higher than that I am afraid nothing can make me go. Believe me profoundly grateful for your painstaking kindness, which I am not in the least likely to forget.

Yours ever sincerely,
L. I. GUINEY.

To E. W. B. Nicholson

6 WINCHESTER ROAD, OXFORD, *May 22,* 1907.

DEAR MR. NICHOLSON,—It won't, I think, be too late to congratulate you on the splendid turn things have taken with regard to the Library? Everybody should realize that the dynamo of it was just you: that long disinterested devotion, the idealism of "a first class fighting man," has sometimes been matched, but not often rewarded, in the world of Oxford. You don't know with what immense sympathy I have gone along with you (not that I count, one way or the other!) and how entirely glad I am at the victorious upshot, all up and down the line. It is as pleasant, almost, to me, as if I had been a subscriber! *Saluti.*

Yours sincerely ever,
LOUISE I. GUINEY.

the house: every stone of it, every shingle of it, every panel and pane of it, laid by Tom's only lily fingers! It took him aeons. But it is done. He celebrated, and became genial, and gave a mediaeval party; I am even informed, by an incredible innuendo of his lady mother's, that Tom was heard to talk!

Now, fare you well, sir, and ever better. I hope all goes well with your beloveds at home. Of my few kinsfolk, I have lost the dearest since I came to England: my great friend and lifelong companion, my poor Aunt Betty, who died in Oxford in 1902. The best of private griefs is that they "break our glass to get more light," and open out vistas, and make one friends with prior and posterior life. To gain such a citizenship is rather comforting, when you know you have made a muddle of your other opportunities in this world.

Your faithful sister and fellow,

L. I. Guiney

[5) S. John's Road, Oxford, is my permanent address, so far as I know it. We leave here in a fortnight. Qualify "we" by dividing it into me and Florence Cocker, once of Cambridge, Massachusetts now of the British Empire nomad and spectator.]

FACSIMILE OF A LETTER TO BRUCE PORTER, DATED HINDERWELL, YORKSHIRE, AUGUST 12, 1903, BY LOUISE IMOGEN GUINEY

To Clement Shorter

6 Winchester Rd., Oxford, *24 May,* [1907.]

Thank you, dear Mr. Shorter, for the letter and enclosure. That fallen star of literature is, to vary the metaphor, a Bad Egg. Still, I don't think he should be hounded so by *Truth.* It is a poor business, on this miserable planet.

I don't wonder at your writing a fifth *Life* of Jane Austen, sure to be the best one. The British Public values you. But fix it in your kind head that it does not want me, and that I have stopped appealing to a general public of any sort. You are the only English editor who will look at verse and prose of mine. I have tried them all: the *Nation* and *Spectator* more than once, because I like them best, but every magazine and weekly at least once. Everything comes back with a printed slip. So I have put in the cork, and hammered it down for good. I would rather have written a *Life* of W. H. than have had a barrel of apples from the Hesperides, any time between 1885 and 1905; but I have long given up the notion on the ground that there is here no general public for me; and nothing can make me change my mind. I am ever so sorry. (I still seem to be good enough for my own country: but of course we are Goths and Vandals.) This is to show you that I am clean out of it all, but grateful as ever for your constant friendship. With affectionate remembrances, yours,

L. I. Guiney.

To Miss Florence A. Crocker

East Hendred, Steventon, Berks, *July 3,* 1907.

Beloved Pal,—I've been thinking of you down here, where I have been for a week. (I fell in love with this village in 1903.) Besides being on high ground as compared with Oxford and environs, it is within three miles or so of the great Downs, across which the Ridgeway runs, *i. e.,* the Romans' Icknield Street. It is a very solitary country, too: everything beautiful on all sides, and the tiny town of Wantage the only thing, nearer than Abingdon, which isn't a wheatfield or a bower of roses. I came down pretty fagged, and haven't picked up very noticeably, owing, I suppose, to the bitter weather. I did nine miles, however, in to-day's rain and wind. Me 'ome is in a cottage, very primitive indeed, but clean as a whistle, with a huge garden and an extremely kind woman to mind it and me. Feather bed, of course! and the faithful cabbage supplying any gap in the chief meal. I have a great mind not to go home on Sat. . . . as I have divers sheets of paper adjacent which I ought to cover with Immortal Works.

I've just been looking at the Staffordshire chart, and thinking of you again: for I wonder how I am going to raise enough for a longish journey (plus lodgment &c.) so soon as the latter half of this month. There is a decent little amount due to me, but it doesn't come in; and I have two obese bills to face before I go out to play. . . .

To Miss Mary A. Jordan

WARREN, ST. IVES, CORNWALL, *11 December,* 1907.

DEAREST MARY,—Whatever will you think, or say? I am one beast. It looks, certainly, as if I wasn't one bit appreciative of that fine Chicago letter, nor of tidings since; and as if I didn't care a hang any more for my blessed Jordans! But you can put every bit of the pigginess down principally to low spirits and inertia, and in a small measure to the fact that for the last six months I have had a great deal of pot-boiling to do: which does certainly connect nausea with a pen! Imagine me as unimaginably out of Oxford. My house-mate is sailing next week for New York, for a visit to her brother; the house isn't closed, and the maids are there: but the winter air in O. is not one bit conducive to work, and it occurred to me to watch out until I could afford the long journey, and then make a dash for Cornwall, a part of the isle I have longed for years to see. Well, I struck luck. I shall stay till Feb. at least. I am lodging cheap, as the lone lodger in a little stone house *in* the sea, with the surf running with all its might straight from Labrador to my window, and wide-eyed gulls sitting on the crest of it (thousands of them,—they're famous at St. Ives!) waiting to share my toast. Anything so perfectly glorious as this air I, certainly, never breathed: for with all its tonic force, it is soft as silk. Here it is December, and my windows are wide open night and day; and I take my constitutional, after scribbling all morning, in such gloves and such a coat as I wear in May at home. There are many pretty sandy coves and beaches on either side of the little harbor, crowded with its tawny sails: in fact, sand is rather a curse hereabouts, however perfect in itself, as the sea is always throwing up "raised beaches" where they are not wanted, and long ago the whole of one town, and part of Lelant, three miles east, disappeared under "towans" as they call them here, of sand. Several very ancient Chapels (6th to 8th century) have been dug out by archæologists: I am going to inspect one of these on Saturday. St. Ives is a bit like Marblehead, only it is built in stone; just so winding, and quaint, and fishy. The narrow lanes have scuppers like a deck; and the flat gray houses have walls nearly four feet thick, and crossbeams like your state-room on a liner. The country inland is not lovely, like Devon, but very bleak: mostly rough moorland, with bouncing dark red streams: no trees to speak of, as the whole district is too wind-swept all the year. The people are dears: kind and intelligent and full of go. The Cymric type is common: dark square strong-shouldered men, with round heads, and eyebrows that might just as well be beards. I discover in local histories that Alice's friends the early Irish overran this whole peninsula and settled here. St. Ives is named for Saint Ia, an Irish princess martyred here by the resident heathen and her brother Saint Uny was a Bishop over towards Hayle. (Aren't the two names perfectly charming? They should be recommended to parents of twins in need of some unhackneyed label.) So I have been at work, as I said, and—what was most startling and unexpected,—the Muse, that jilt whom I have not seen to speak to once a year since 1900, suddenly turned up, grinning, and clad in seaweed! If you are by way of seeing the *Atlantic* or *McClures,* the results, or some of them, will show up there. *McClure* is a great patron of mine lately, always asking for those masterpieces which are the delight of the civilized world! (By the way, I must tell you my income from "litturachoor" in printed books for 1907 is exactly one shilling. Fact. Hooray!) I am sending an illustrated paper. The coloured picture which ought to go with it can't, as it is four or five inches longer than the roll: I am most reluctantly bestowing it on my excellent landlady, who keeps me fat on fresh herring and clotted cream, taken "not simultaneous but consecutive," as has been said of wives. I wish I had something worth while to post you each for a Merry Christmas, which I wish you with all my heart. As I am writing to *meine Mutter* tonight also, I will wind up, with heaps of love to Mother Jordan, Alice, and "dear old" Mary. I hope all the family flourish, and that the little folk are happy and well. Mam seems to have a plan to go back to Auburndale next summer or autumn, and would like me to fall in. Of course if she really wants me, back I come; but a move into a now furnitureless house, or a taking up of the difficulties of housekeeping there, seems to me most impracticable. I do not know whether you have run across a rather nice fifty-year-old cousin of mine, who is living with her on Massachusetts Avenue?

I have been doing several articles for the new *Cath. Encyclopaedia.* Fancy me at that trade! Chaucer is done; and they have asked me to do Crashaw. Vaughan, etc.—my own work, that is—is hung up.

Yours affectionately,

LOU.

To Wilfrid Meynell

C/o MRS. GRENFELL, WARREN, ST. IVES, CORNWALL,
12 *Dec.*, 1907.

DEAR MR. MEYNELL,—Thank you a thousand times: I am so sadly proud to have that![1] and I am making bold to beg particularly, if I may, for two more. One is for our Rector, Fr. Arthur Day, S. J., at Oxford, who dearly loves Mr. Thompson's poems, and once read "The Hound of Heaven" to the Beaumont boys, throughout, during a Retreat he was giving. He will be sure to put it in his Breviary, and to put him into many and many a prayer. You blessed Meynells! Who but you would have chosen that touching line, and remembered to replace the King of Sorrows which one often finds on a memorial card by this unique and beautiful print? Your *Athenæum* article, with that knightly touch near the end, hit me very hard. What a thing you have done, you two, for England and for the Faith! and what benedictions will lie in wait for you, and dog your memories, centuries hence!

> "—*In cima all 'erto e faticoso colle*
> *Della Virtù riposto è il vostro bene.*"

I am here for a few weeks, in a cottage placidly seated *in* the pounding sea. Sweeter winter air never

[1] Memorial card of Francis Thompson.

blew: it does blow, though! There's a five-year-old Mission, most edifying. My love as ever to the only Catholic poet left who counts.

Yours most sincerely,
L. I. GUINEY.

To Florence A. Crocker

[Early in 1908.]

DEAR OLD LASS,—It was so jolly to get your nice note, plus that scrumptiously good cake from your Oxford *Mutterchen!* I have been off for a week, partly rooting in an excellent Reference Library at Penzance, partly wandering in and out of ancient villages, as I needed the exercise after many weeks' pretty steady work. I saw pleasant things: rainbows, wild primroses, and periwinkles, sturdy women postmen, and other flora and fauna. Roads muddy, but skies blue. I do so like these alert brown-eyed Cornish folk. As you eat your evening rhubarb and cream, they give you matrimonial advice—"'Appy as 'ee are, Miss? Well, don't 'ee get a man if 'ee don't want 'un. But *if* 'ee gets 'un, *keep they under!*" The women are no crushed minority at the Lizard and the Land's End! They are full of fire and impetus, these Britons of the real stock. They can all sing, and they can all cook. I get much amusement and exhilaration out of them.

I am delighted that you are getting on. Long live the "snail's pace"! I'm not so sure but that it is the best of all paces. Your handiwork embraces me (though with increasing difficulty!) daily. I wish you were as well as I am—not a nerve humming. *Auf wiedersehen! Ihre dichliebende*

L.

To The Rev. Arthur F. Day, S. J.

123 KILLIGREW ROAD, FALMOUTH, [*4 March,* 1908.]
(*Ash Wednesday*)

DEAREST FATHER,—I do so appreciate your having sent me the card from Newbury. And somehow, it has a hopeful sound. With this better weather, and sunshine, that very dear invalid ought to mend, D. V. Indeed, I can well understand the blessed comfort to you of his having got down to Mass. He is always in my mind. I think I never told you how in June last when Lady Day came up in the motor to E. Hendred, and carried me and Laurie Cameron, who was there that day, to lunch at Falkland Lodge, Sir John, long silent, turned to me with—and if he hadn't looked so earnest, I should have laughed a bit:—

"Does my Arthur do *any* GOOD in Oxford?" So I gave you a "character" which seemed to satisfy him sufficiently well. I so liked this: his whole anxiety, to see you acquit yourself before the Lord. My own young Father once wrote to me when I was twelve, and away at School: "If you fail, I fail in you." And he was very much like a Day; and his handwriting so oddly like your own.

All is well with me. In this Diocese (perhaps elsewhere?) fasting, save for today and Good Friday, is abrogated: you can't much mind if I toe the mark, together with all the world, for these two days? I have been grumbling unconscionably about the cold: mollycoddle! Despite it, the country is wonderfully beautiful, and there are already plenty of primroses. I should have loved to stay longer *Chez notre soeur,* but I have such a heap of editing on the poet Vaughan (ob. 1695) to do, that six or seven full weeks is due at least to him. *Tu vale et me ama in Xto.* Send me a marconigraph Lenten blessing.

Oh! . . . an idea. Would Sir John be able to eat some very extra good oysters, those from the Helford River bed near here? I should delight in sending some. Not much labour to eat an oyster. As ever, dear Father,

L. I. G.

To Bertram Dobell

123 KILLIGREW ROAD, FALSMOUTH, *13 March,* 1908.

DEAR MR. DOBELL,—You spoil me! I am delighted to have the book, and thank you most heartily for it. Your Preface is so "right"! One does have to laugh at dear *little* Shelley, not only at nineteen but at twenty-nine too, for his excessive, romantic faith in trousers and petticoats. Never was such a believer born into the world. If he had lived till the Oxford Movement, he would have been "the noblest 'Roman'"! Elizabeth Hitchener, take her all in all, was a much nicer person than Emilie Viviani. Why do you fall foul of women-kind for not liking "Platonics"? That proves that you are no American, doesn't it?

I once found in Ireland, in possession of a lady who

had positively no literary sense, the guidebook which Shelley bought in Dublin out of that dole of pocket-money which Eliza Westbrook allowed him, and in which he had written his name and scored down an itinerary. I got Dr. Garnett to buy it, for the Br. Mus. It used to be in the showcases. You have no idea how devoted I am to Shelley, these twenty years. Every Shelleyan ought to thank you for making Mr. [Thomas James] Wise's *trouvaille* into a general heirloom.

It struck me the other day that it would be scrumptious of you to give us a book to be called *Three Essays on the Dramatic Spirit:* Dryden's Dramatick Poesy, 1665, leading: then two very fine, and almost utterly unknown papers following: George Farquhar on Comedy, and Richard West's long Preface to his own translation of Hecuba, printed in 1726. This was the Chancellor West, son-in-law of Bp. Burnet, and father to his name-sake son who was so dear to Gray. These would really make a most interesting and rather Dobellian book. Do consider the possibility of such a reprint.

If I can manage it (and all my ifs are purely financial for ever), I am going to spend some weeks in Cambridge this summer. Not to lose so good a chance I shall do some digging in the University Library, on behalf of our friend Alabaster. And if I can get up courage enough, when the time comes, I'll beg you to lend me your original MS. to collate with the one Mr. Sayle copied. *Placetne?* I like it much here. Nice air to sit and slog in. With love and gratitude,

L. I. G.

To Florence A. Crocker

123 KILLIGREW RD., FALMOUTH, *18 March,* 1908.

My Zoul! WhatEVER! Bless your dear old heart for a maker of Christmas in the middle of Lent. I didn't even know you could create such beauties, and am so lost in admiration of 'em that Thank You comes last, instead of first. The colours are a delight. I don't like to tread on them, and have been speculating on the question of wearing one shoe on either ear, while the chilly weather lasts, outdoors! Really, you "ingeniose devill" of friendship, I am as pleased as ever I can be, and immensely grateful. But—my zoul! How could you? Me!!!

I slog at it, as Stevenson so classically remarks, every day, and begin to see land. The incessant mud keeps me from my usual late afternoon explorations; but there are acres of oleanders and rhododendrons in bloom all about, despite the cold. You would be perfectly happy with my landlady, yclept Grant, in this sweet place: put her down on your list. She is a wonder for neatness, promptness, and kind painstaking to the limit, and, as all the Cornish women are, a good cook. One thing disappoints me here. The two Libraries are rather a sell, so far as I am concerned: to get at *any* "scholars' books," even the *Dict. Nat. Biography* and *Notes and Queries,* I have to travel back to Penzance. I am running over there tonight . . . Much sitting does not tend to my contraction, and I am almost bursting out of the invaluable "bodies" which you presented to my mortality! . . . Be you monstrous careful of one F. A. C. Ever with love,

L. I. G.
(a Calced Carmelite.)[1]

To Edmund Gosse

6 WINCHESTER ROAD, OXFORD, *June 10,* 1908.

DEAR MR. GOSSE,—You will be weary of compliments and salaams! but as I have only just read *Father and Son,* I am late in crying out how good it is, and how unreservedly I have enjoyed it. "Good" is hardly the word for a book of so many entrancing perfections: it is perfect art, I think, and perfect taste, tone and feeling. Even anonymity is, for once, a perfection! There is a sort of gallant sweetness about both the pathos and the humour of it all which pairs off with many a page of R. L. S. (Did I ever tell you, by the way, what Isobel Strong once told me, that he certainly loved you the very best of all his friends?) To save me, I cannot help thanking you for that exquisite *biographie à deux.* It reminds me, all over again, to be proud of an old belief in its author, and an old affection for him and his works and his pomps.

I spent the whole winter in Cornwall and Devon. Alas! they are, as you recall to us, scraped shores, in more cases than one. But there is no such air elsewhere.

For the rest I am a real Oxford anchoress, and have

[1] The Discalced Carmelites are a monastic Order who go barefoot: from *calceus*, shoe.

not seen London for years! My love to dear Mrs. Gosse, and Tessa, Philip and Sylvia.

Yours as ever,
LOUISE I. GUINEY.

To George Norton Northrop

14 WINCHESTER ROAD, *Oct. 17,* [? 1908.]

MY DEAR POET,—How nice of you! I prize it [Gerald Gould's *Poems*] tremenjous. I think the lyric you pointed out, and the little one which ends

"The blackbirds sang with one consent
In the green leaves of May,"

are the top notch. Sonnets beautiful and "straight," too, and excellence of an astonishingly mature kind on every page. All so amazingly modern in tone, moreover: owing nothing to myths, historical association, or even religion, although no whit lacking in the natural religiousness of poetry, and full of a sadness never bitter. How does the childie hit off, in the matters of technique and concentration of thought, what an honest writer might very well spend forty years in slaving for? He is a miracle. T. Whittemore has gone to London with the book in his pocket. He liked you immensely, and Mr. Moulton too: so I hope you took to him? He will be back next week, and will be in Oxford a great deal during the winter.

Do you know that I'd like to put you on a gallon of milk and six eggs per day, plus whatever else you would eat? Why do you look so transparent? "O reform it altogether!" I do most heartily hope friendly concern is wasted, and that you are much better than you seem. But be careful, little brother in Apollo. Accept my thanks and affectionate good wishes, meanwhile, for Gerald Gould his Workes.

Yours ever,
L. I. GUINEY.

To Bruce Porter

AUBURNDALE, MASSACHUSETTS, *Jan. 26,* [1909.]

MY DEAR BRUCE PORTER,—Think of the adventures of the delectable bookie (did you edit it?) which you sent me: first waylaid in Wyoming, and disembowelled partly with fire; then limping over to Oxford: next painfully chasing me, who left England on New Year's Eve, back to this dull Auburndale. Only today has it fallen upon my neck with a gurgle as of a homing pigeon. *Alleliebster Bruder,* I thank you well. Moreover, the thing itself has life in it: I shall love it when I come to read it through. With somewhat gingerly handling, that can easily be done.

How has it gone with you since we were out together in the Oxford Sunday rains? Miss Anderson is in Sussex now, and the Andrews family have migrated from Bryn Mawr to John Hopkins. If you have been by way of seeing *McClure's,* you will have seen frequent eruptions of my unaccountable Muse in that otherwise respectable purlieu: but all that is over. Now for godliness! You wouldn't know me, with no end of unsymbolic adiposity accumulating over against my lean mind! If ever you come again to Boston, you will be welcome in these rural wilds. Mrs. Williams would remember 'em. What does, what will, what must she think of me for a doomb deil? Fare you well, and all blessings dog your way! One of my reasons for loving you dear is your shameless fashion of recognizing that blessings do happen, and happen, moreover, in dog-and-cat showers. I am ever so glad you remember me yet.

Your old friend,
L. I. GUINEY.

To George Norton Northrop

MAINE, [*Summer,* 1909.]

MY POET DEAR,—The aristocratic-looking volume [*In Itinere*], with its delightful inscription, has found me in farthest Maine. I write to thank you for it, sitting on the rocks, in close propinquity to a pounding surf; so if there be splashes on this page, the same will not be tears. Besides, why weep over so pleasant a gift? Didn't you delete several Noble Numbers? I seem to miss a good many. And there's one I like but never saw before: the lines to Alan Stevenson. Who is he? Son to that wonderful all-alive R. A. M. S., who is absurdly reported as long dead? I hope so. I thought, and still think, the Magdalen group of sonnets ought to be together. May the bookie have luck, and get loved! for it is good art and honest handicraft. I am gratified that you fulfilled your dream of publishing a book of verses while you were at Magdalen . . . Did I tell you that Houghton, Mifflin and Co. are doing me in swagger style this Autumn? Limited edition and a'. I call the book *Happy Ending,* as it is an omnium gatherum: and as the name enrages some of my too optimistic friends.

Isn't it horrid to miss you? We that might sit under an Auburndale willow and weep for

"That towery city, branchy between towers!"

Alack! We have sold our Auburndale property; and I have been in three Maine purlieus, a-visiting, and am just now hanging on to the edge of the New Brunswick border. The town is pretty, and eke the country-side; but what a hurried, sketchy, impermanent look it all has! Does that ever affect you as it does me? and the mosquito is putting on his war bonnet. I am glad to hear of your University of Wisconsin appointment, and of your nefarious but concealed project to [return] to Oxford as fast as a fresh state of circumstances will permit. *Ego quoque*. . . .

Remember me to Messrs. Gould, Meynell (if "up"!), Thomas, Clarke, and Bosworth. T. W. seems to be Gallicanising at a great rate. He is not a geographical Unitarian, like me. *Saluti.*

Yours as ever,
LOUISE I. GUINEY.

To Clement Shorter

41 PARK ST., HOULTON, MAINE, *21 July,* [1909.]

Dear Mr. Shorter, your little letter, addressed to Oxford, has just reached me. As to my address, it is literally, at the present moment, nothing much more definite than the Western Hemisphere, 42° No. Lat., or thereabouts. You see we have lately sold our old home: yet anything sent to Auburndale, Boston, Masstts., will be forwarded, I fancy, for many a year to come! I expect to stay where I now am (on a visit to my elderly cousins) until September 15th. Your saying that you will "write no more just now" means, I trust, that I shall hear further from you in the near future: welcome alternative! I never had enough yet of Dora, or of you; and my dog-like trick of inhabiting holes when I am not in a grinning good humour, won't blind either of you to the fact that old love and gratitude are things in me which will never change.

Mind you don't ask me whether I miss Oxford and Oxfordshire! Joy be with you in Knockmoroon. Tell Dora I am getting as obese as Dinizulu.

Ever yours,
L. I. GUINEY.

To Aleck Abrahams

41 PARK ST., HOULTON, MAINE, *6 Sept.*, 1909.

Dear Aleck, you are a wonder for efficiency-cum-kindness! I hope you had a first-rate time at Whitleaf, a place unknown to me, who have haunted Cotswolds rather than Chilterns. I have acquired a lively interest in Whitleaf because of your description of its natural *and* financial charms, and if I ever break gaol, so to speak, shall look it up. The police post-card came duly, and Edw. forwarded me the nice one which reported your Bucks jaunt with one L. A. [his sister]. *Our* bobbies are hideous over here: they can't run a step for fat, and few have civil tongues. I lost my heart to the Lunnon force long ago.

I revel in the Cromwellian notes you sent me: so many, and all so pertinent! This brewer ancestry is quite a new thing to me. Surely very noticeable, those five malted progenitors: probably gatherers of much of the wealth which set up the family, and shoved it by Qu. Elizabeth's time into full "gentleness." The Tangye quotation is valuable, whatever the context may be. I daresay there are other grounds than the Thomason ballad for saying the early Royalists called Oliver and his father brewers. I have in my day run over dozens of Royalists sketches of the regicides &c., and ought to remember a slur of that sort; but unluckily I don't. Of course I must prove that Oliver was occupying some palace or other by 1646. I feel sure he didn't take up residence at Hampton Court until considerably later. Vaughan yaps at Oliver, as was natural, in at least two other (by-his-editors-unidentified) places. How they loved, in the sweet old days, to harp on any personal shortcoming real or imagined, physical or intellectual! Our manners really are somewhat better in such respects. I thank you heartily for both your fine packets of notes, and especially for the friendly but almost too self-sacrificing resolve of digging further!

If you are within call of the Bodleian (if not, there is not the remotest haste about the business), would you look up two little old books by Sir John Hayward, one on Elizabeth's reign, one on James I's right to the throne, and run down a passage relating to Qu. Mary Stuart's trial, in which there is some mention of Dr. William Awbrey, one of the judge-commissioners favourable to her? I much want to know what is said of him there. These books are not in Boston libraries. What do you make of this (Vaughan again):

"Learning and Law, your day is done,
And your work too: you may be gone! . . .
Bold vice and blindness now dare act,
And *like the grey groat* pass, though crack'd."

This in lines on the death of Judge Arthur Trevor, who died in 1666. I understand the groat to have been a silver coin, fourpence. But why "grey," and why "pass, though crack'd"? Of course any coin of the realm might so do. What was Vaughan's spite against the groat? Had that worthy object any special history, *temp. Car. II.*? "Blindness" reminds me to tell you that H. V. has an unmistakable (to me) reference to Milton's total blindness, in 1655; and another to his oncoming blindness in 1646. I am going to dish these up for the *Athenaeum* some day. My pious poet was "a good hater," if ever there was one.

My cousin took me off on a spree last week, over the border into New Brunswick, and the splendid valley of the St. John. It had been raining hard for days, and the great Falls were magniffy. . . .

Your much-beholden,
L. I. G.

To Clement Shorter

AUBURNDALE, BOSTON, MASSTTS., U. S. A.,
27 Sept., 1909.

EVER DEAR MR. SHORTER,—My publishers over here, Houghton Mifflin and Co., are going to publish a digest of my poetic *opera omnia,* in very handsome style, before Christmas.[1] I do not know how extensive an effort they mean to make in presenting the outpourings

[1] *Happy Ending.*

of my incomparable genius to the English public; but at any rate, they want to place out about a score of copies for review, in any quarter where those who would like such wares may be found. Now I have been too long out of London to draw up such a list; some of my best men-at-arms, like Dr. Garnett and dear Lionel, are gone; some others I hesitate to suggest as possible victims: *e. g.*, Mr. Lang, whom I never met, but who has been ever so kind to me. You see my point: it is that I wish you would give me some names for H. M. and Co. Nobody will know better than you the men whom the twang of my individual harp can reach: I am quite aware that for better and for worse, I am not everybody's poeticule!

It is a satisfaction to be let loose on a general revise of one's work, at last. I am gathering only lyrics, and eliminating not a few. The enclosed, a rune of beasts, is for the greatest beast-lover I know: I fancy she will not have seen it? Love to her. Be sure any advice of yours will go far.

Yours always,
L. I. GUINEY.

To Clement Shorter

21st Oct., 1909.

DEAR MR. SHORTER,—Please take my most hearty thanks for the nice list you have sent me. I shall pass it over at once to my publishers, who will be delighted to act accordin'. Only I have taken the liberty to cancel Mr. [William] Archer's name, as I have been told he dislikes my work. He left me out, you may remember, of his anthology; but in such highly delectable company (Lionel's, Mme. Darmesteter's, &c.) that I forgave him on the instant. Of course I shall add your and Mr. Hutchinson's[1] names to the catalogue of victims. Not that I want either of you to bother with any such thing as a review! In either case, it is just a very small acknowledgment of long-appreciated kindness to my Muse, poor old baggage!

"Why am I not in Oxford?" and "Why was I not better disposed while I was there, to loyal friends?" I suppose you don't know at all how these questions hurt? these questions with their one accursed basis of *haute finance*? I am not "wandering" over the States now, either; but I have just ended a six-months' absence from Boston, most of it passed in a decorous visit to a Maine cousin. My new address (I think I told you we had sold out at Auburndale?) is 42 Pinckney St., Boston. No: I really can't bear to be teased on the subject of my friends far away, most of whom I had to give up seeing much of after 1902. It is a sore subject: for I love them well and ever. *De te fabula.* Adore Dora for me; and believe me most gratefully yours,

L. I. GUINEY.

To Rev. J. J. Burke, C. S. P.,[2]

42 PINCKNEY ST., BOSTON, *Nov. 8,* 1909.

DEAR FR. BURKE,—. . . I think my old friend Miss [Agnes] Repplier and myself would have enjoyed it

[1] Editor of the *Windsor Magazine.*

[2] Editor of the *Catholic World,* New York.

more if we had known we were to demolish Fr. Talbot Smith between us! And why didn't you print us *seriatim*? Her article is first-rate; better than mine for several reasons, and not least that it is more personal. (I see she puts *me* among the "successes"! but I never yet wrote a book which financially was even the ghost of a success. My income from all of them isn't $15 per annum!! However, her chief point is that the secular reading world do not blackball authors known to be Catholic; nor do they.)

I had the pleasure, lately, of meeting Frs. Younan and Moran. It made me wish all over again that there were Paulists in heathen Boston, come to stay. Isn't this fine news from Garrison, N. Y.? I hope they won't put out their "Anglo-Roman" *Lamp*, though it can be fed now with real holy oil.

Hoping that you keep well, dear Father,

Yours ever,
L. I. GUINEY.

To The Rev. Arthur F. Day, S. J.

Dec. 15, 1909.

DEAREST FATHER,—With all most affectionate Christmas wishes, I send you under separate cover a book published two days ago, with which you have already been threatened.[1] I want you to see it, and perhaps look it over with some interest, for the sake of what begins to be auld lang syne: but you need not feel obliged to keep it. You must keep, I think, better things of mine than a book? *e. g., cor meum in Christo;* and much

[1] Happy Ending.

do I covet that you shall hang on to that, until it gets Home, *ahead* of Your Reverence, I hope! There are over twenty things in the book which were written during your Oxford consulship, some while I was in Cornwall. Those on pp. 44, 51, 82, 118, 132, I think I have shown you; but please look now at 121 [1] (and the note to it especially—it was you who made me sure of the pimpernel in that wonderful field near Appleton) and then look at 113 [2] which I never told anyone, not even you, was writ during your first month or two at St. A.'s, before I hardly knew you at all, and aimed directly at you! After all these years, as there is nothing to change or recall in the general sentiment, I print it. Just be glad, quite impersonally, (as you so easily can, and so often are) that you were that much of an uplift to me in the very beginning, when I was in the shadow of my dear Aunt Betty's death. P. 34 [3] is, so to speak, a Winchester Rd. poem; and p. 35 [4] my revenge, in a way, on . . . [certain] non-lovers; and p. 36 [5] is a queer little thing invisibly dated from Iffley. (I am not going to bestow all this valuable information on others, be sure.) Isn't it a beauteous book to look at? The edition is limited, and the price high. The rarely reproduced Watts frontispiece is the joy of my life. I have always seen in that picture my whole philosophy of life, and planned long ago to use it, and to connect it in some way with the verses by no means worthy of it. Hence

[1] "A Footpath Morality."
[2] "To One who would not Spare Himself."
[3] "Cobwebs."
[4] "Astræa."
[5] "The Yew-Tree."

the title, an invention of my own already being reviled by my friends; and hence the eight lines (mine too) under the photogravure, in 18th century style. But I am "burbling" about the rhymes more than is meet, and must cease.

I am mightily pleased at your having 1, kept the blue rug a whole year; and 2, given it to good old Willy. . . .

Blessing on you, dear, dear Father! Keep well. Think of me a little when you kneel at the Crib, and when you bless the children on or about Holy Innocents' Day; and also at Epiphany-day-after when another birthday pops up to reprove me, like Stevenson's bird, who

> "—cocked his shining eye and said:
> *Ain't* you 'shamed, you Sleepy-head!"

Things continue to go on ever so well, *laus Deo*. Please don't write until you are thoroughly rested from all the fatigues of the great Feasts.

Your ever devoted,

L. I. G.

To Miss Elizabeth Abrahams

42 PINCKNEY ST., BOSTON, U. S. A., *Dec. 29,* 1909.

DEAREST LIZZIE,— . . . Of course Aleck will have got the book? I should have written as well, for I want to fight him for a groat. Tell him the information which he so scornfully rejects about groats not being coined after 1662, comes from that mine of all scholarly accuracy, the New English Dictionary! True, a fourpenny piece was issued in early Victorian days, though it was not, I think? *officially* a groat; but at any rate there was evidently a long gap in the minting of the ancient groat. The same omniscient N. E. D. under "grey" defines a "grey groat" as a worthless affair, symbolical of all contemptuous disvaluation, like "I don't care a brass farthing." I fancy this was exactly Vaughan's meaning. If Aleck, by the way, is as efficient as a housemate and brother as he is as a ferret, you are in an enviable case, and I share your profits.

George and Rachel [Norton] were here together the other day, but I haven't seen the family for weeks. The [Christmas] down-town and house decorations are perfectly beautiful in the snow, most of the wreaths and great garlands being hung outside. Your recollection of steep Pinckney St. is correct. I am at the top of the hill, where it is still extremely quiet and old-fashioned. The Common is but a minute's walk around the corner. Happy New Year, all hands round! Ever yours with much affection,

L. I. G.

To The Rev. J. J. Burke, C. S. P.

75 PLEASANT ST., NEWTON CENTRE,[1] MASS., *March 1,* 1910.

DEAR FR. BURKE,—I seem to be plaguing you with almost daily letters! Well, you see your unfailing goodness draws it upon you. Convalescence seems to be a

[1] On February 5th, 1910, at the age of 80, Mrs. Guiney died, rather suddenly. L. I. G., who had not been well before this event and became seriously ill afterwards, made her home for some weeks with Dr. Alice M. Jackman, of Newton Centre, where skilful care restored her sufficiently to enable her to sail for England in May. The cousins referred to in the letter did not join her until 1911 and 1912, respectively.

great time for thinking, I find: and I have been thinking hard on many topics. You know already how I want a summer's open-airing, a needed rest, Over There? There are two young girl-cousins of mine, orphans, whom I am bent upon *sousing* in the atmosphere of a Catholic country, to wit, Belgium: they need it badly. The elder would gladly go as my secretary. . . . the younger will be at a Benedictine school, if God prospers the plan as we now lay it, but living with a family in town, not (probably) at the Convent. You see the details are vague. But this detail isn't—that I have a great mind to ask you whether you would allow her to write a monthly letter to *The Leader?* She is not much past fourteen, but has a particularly level young head, with observation, humor, and a distinct turn for wording things in a natural, bright, and childishly interesting way. I don't know that you would care at all to encourage my idea, especially as I want her to be paid for her letters, if they pass muster. But my root idea is not pocket money (they're poor, and have been rich!): it is gripping on to a strong Catholic interest, inseparable *at first* from self-interest, just as I want it to be. . . . I certainly think that if she were started on a series of short letters aimed at her own much-loved brother of sixteen, something not uninteresting to *The Leader's* young following might result. All this not to begin before October. What do you think? Don't stretch a point to gratify me, but tell me true at your leisure. . . .

Pray for me. *Saluti.*

Yours ever, dear Father,

L. I. GUINEY.

To Bertram Dobell

ASHBOURNE, DERBYSHIRE, *June 16,* 1910.

DEAR MR. DOBELL,—Your ever kind letter got no earlier reply, because I was preparing to return to England: "for ever" as Shelley liked to say. And now here I am, much in love with this sweet little Dovedale town, and not likely to settle again in Oxford until Michaelmas or after. Meanwhile, I shall be in London for some weeks, and of course I will run in to see with my own eyes how you are; and here is a hope to find you as well as I would have you! As to the dedication which in your extreme goodness you threaten me with, shouldn't I be as proud as a peacock and as pleased as Punch!?!

This last year, marked for me by the loss of my dear Mother and a long disconcerting illness of my own, has brought my work to a standstill, but I am full of new plans, and feeling very well, at present. I must show you sometime our friend Alabaster's pedigree which I have compiled, showing his kinship to Bp. Still of *Gammer Gurton's Needle,* and to John Winthrop, first Governor of the Province of Massachusetts Bay. I shall pursue that cryptic gentleman's poetry very much further, I trust, before 1910 ends.

With affectionate wishes and remembrances, dear Mr. Dobell, I am,

Yours always,

L. I. GUINEY.

To Aleck Abrahams

ASHBOURNE, DERBY, *June 28,* 1910.

MY DEAR ALECK,—Thou'rt ten Angels. I treasure the parochial information, and return you the card, as requested. I should be much delighted to get my eagle eye upon all those registers *circa* 1650-8, on the chance of running across Thomas and Rebecca Vaughan. Meanwhile (as you put me up to more impositions!) wilt look in Carlyle or any other likely book for a *personal description* of Oliver Protector? I know the mole, &c.; but what I want to know is 1, whether he had a muddy complexion; and 2, *red,* noticeably *red,* lips? If so, Vaughan is hitting at him in another hitherto unnoticed poem. I long to find out, but this county hasn't a book in it! Last week I went to the Salt Library in Stafford. This might be quite splendidly valuable, if there were any catalogue at all representing what is now on the shelves, and if everything were not thrown about on or under tables and chairs! It is really miserably sad to see such disorder and confusion. There's a learned old Librarian, very kind; but he was at sea, and so was I.

Ashbourne and neighbourhood continue to strike me as perfectly adorable. Prices are ditto, compared to Oxford.

Tell one L. A. that I love her dear.

Yours ever,

L. I. G.

To Bertram Dobell

ASHBOURNE, *July 9,* 1910.

DEAR MR. DOBELL,—When you give me a choice between your very own book, and a book, however, excellent, by James Thomson, of course you know I should take the first? as is human and natural, criticism or comparison apart. I'd rather wait for it, too, than have the other now.

I am by no means a wildly enthusiastic Whitmanite, though I love the bigness and upgatherishness (if one may coin such a fearsome word!) of Walt's spirit. But his formlessness kills him for me, as a poet. Vastly should I appreciate it, if, when you come to it, you would just say "my friend L. I. G., &c.," which is what I hope I am; and let all the noble adjectives go hang! Besides, they might look a bit overstrained: for who in England, beyond my own private circle, reads the silver-toned undersigned? But if I figure as a friend of Mr. Dobell's, I shall have done well indeed. Ever so many thanks, and most lively good wishes from

L. I. G.

To Mary Winefride Day

36 Charles St., Iffley Road, Oxford,
Sunday eve, Autumn 1910.

My very dear Mary,—Your measures are good, heaped up and running over, when you do "pay up"! so don't fret about times and seasons. I like to hear whenever I do hear, and for the rest, you are to do as you please, or as occasions and circumstances at Bryndart please; and I shall never love you a whit the less. A doggie! And 'Fonso's nose actually not out of joint, either! Isn't that a most delicate breed to try to rear in this country? You have given him the obvious local name, I see; but could there be a better one for the light-footed greyhounds? As a prodigious lover of dogs, and an old, old hand at bringing up puppies, will you let me say that I have half a fear you are developing this infant's emotional faculties too fully? You will smile at this. But you know what I mean. A dog's heart has a power of loving quite beyond the normal human capacity, and then, you really are a very nice missis, as Dart has already discovered. But if he claims you practically every minute, and weeps and wails whenever you leave him, he is laying up a great deal of unnecessary pain for his little self in the future, and some bother and anxiety for the so-entirely-with-all-his-soul-adored lady, to drop into German! Oh my! how I did cherish my darling old St. Bernards, big as calves before they came to the jacket-and-trousers age! and two of them in particular, father and son, were lovers like Dart, making me their sun, moon, and candle light; and I had to argue them out of a great deal of it. I can still see my dear sighing Brontë take his paw from my hand when I began: "Come, now! Be a Manly Dog!" and proceeded to put on my hat and go to the station, with all his eyes fixed on the back of my head. And there were earthquakes and avalanches of joy when I got back. But it is quite easy to teach them to be philosophers, and never whimper. Poor little velvety chap, I hope he won't find it a very cold winter. You should be quite happy with a house to your mind, and your young niece holding her own, thanks to your splendid care, and two sweet pets, and the wonderful "Dayite" Gertrude (of whom I have heard) to stoke your ship for you. It is even nicer than Lynton, don't you think? Oh, how very much I should like to pass that week with you! It is dear of you to ask me. I could have wished you hadn't, because I don't like to say what is true, that I can't manage it, alas! You see I leave here (or expect to, I should say) on the 21st, and go to London until the 26th with half-a-dozen necessitous things to do, such as all-alone people have to see to for themselves.

Christmas Day falls on Sunday this year, so I can make that a visit to some old friends in Kensington. And then I must just fly post-haste to my Falmouth work, having already lost a whole mortal month (owing to an indisposition in Bruges) out of my planned winter. I am so sorry, and I send you a round of affectionate thanks; very rueful and wishful thanks they are.

I am miles from St. Aloysius, but very near the new Church-to-be, SS. Edmund and Frideswide, which looks very promising architecturally, though built of rubble and sandstone, with a brick interior! My rooms, and the landlady and her ways, are perfection. I wonder if Somebody will ever, like Fr. Wilson, be sent back to Oxford, to tempt you here again? It is so gratifying to know the Preston staff has been strengthened. But then I feel quite as you do, that the long and short of it is that Preston is no place for him. Goodnight. Ever so much love from

Yours always,
L. I. GUINEY.

To Clement Shorter

RAMSGATE, *Nov. 4,* 1910.

MY DEAR MR. SHORTER,—They have made my great friend Miss Morgan Mayor of Brecon. (The local enthusiasm is immense. G. is a Liberal, read herself into Liberalism when young.) Do you remember once asking me for a few paragraphs about her? "On that hint I spake." I have written the enclosed at top speed, but perhaps you can work it into the *Sphere,* and send her a copy? The address is Buckingham Place, Brecon, So. Wales. She is, as you know, a great admirer of your books; and if you care to ask her at once for a photograph just taken (her only one in years) and data for a biographical notice, you'll get them, and at once. This is quite an event to me. I do not think I have over-praised her.

I came back to England (Derbyshire) last May. In late July I passed through London, and the first thing I did was to go up to Dora's door: but even the gate was locked, and there was no sign of a caretaker within, so I had to flee away. I was en route for Bruges, to place a little cousin at school, or rather to arrange for her placing, and Bruges didn't agree with me, and I got miserable and sleepless again, until this nice Ramsgate (ever so nice when quite deserted) set me up. I hope to go up to Oxford very soon now. But I shall stay in West Hampstead for a day or two while I do some abhorred shopping, and if you are both in town again, I should so like to see you. (I shall stay with an old friend, Miss Abrahams, sister to the young antiquary and topographer of that name who adorns the pages of *Notes and Queries,* and, I think, has a slight acquaintance with you?) Make my peace with Dora, whom I owe for a sweet letter, this long while. She may not know that I have been ill and in all sorts of trouble; but I fancy I am quite re-established at last. However, I am more of a hermit than ever: my old friends must all forgive me for that. It implies no diminution of my love for them. I hope all goes well with you both, and with both your families.

Yours ever,

L. I. GUINEY.

To The Rev. J. J. Burke, C. S. P.

OXFORD, *2 December,* [1910.]

DEAR FR. BURKE,—There isn't a ghost of an idea in my head yet, to form any nucleus for future *C. W.* articles, but I have a suggestion to make, quite disconnected with my own work. A friend of mine [Thomas Whittemore] is editing for publication in the Spring, (with my help) the prose papers of Lionel Johnson. They are all here now, under my hand; Miss Johnson has given me complete control of them. The book has to be for a general public, so naturally all the Catholic things cannot go in. But they are so good, so sane, so masterfully written, some of these brief essays, that I am wondering whether you would like to use them? I enclose a little list of titles. I must tell you that they have been printed: mostly in a very literary weekly called the *Anti-Jacobin,* which circulated even here among the smallest possible clientèle, and died early; the others in the *Daily Chronicle,* which naturally has no chance of being read in America. The dates range between 1894 and 1899. It may be considered absolutely certain, especially as regards the American

Catholic public, that these papers are as unknown as if they still lay in MS. If you wish to print them, they are yours: and the honorarium may be anything you please, or nothing! All Miss Johnson counts upon are a few copies of *C. W.* if you decide affirmatively. (She is not a Catholic: Lionel was the only one of his family to enter the Church.) This will reach you at a busy season, but I shall hope to hear from you fairly soon. I give only my London address, as I shall soon be leaving Oxford for my winter's work in Cornwall.

Every best wish to you, dear Father Burke.

Yours faithfully,
L. I. GUINEY.

P. S. I find a few come from the *Academy*. Of course there is no question of copyright.

To Prof. George Herbert Palmer

OXFORD, *11 Dec.,* 1910.

MY DEAR PROFESSOR PALMER,—I wish you the merriest kind of a Christmas, and I wish you had that first edition Carew to help make it so! I often think of you and the dear books, especially now that I am so much in Bodley again. It is a friendly climate, Bodley: but outside, it has poured steadily for sixteen days. Of course that means floods, and picturesque they certainly are, making of Oxford a seacoast array of spires and pinnacles. I am off to Falmouth for the winter, and for my final work on Herbert his parodist and adorer.[1]

[1] Henry Vaughan.

Miss Morgan and I have planned this for long; but what do you think? They have made that gentle book-woman and philanthropist Mayor of Brecon! and alas, I shoulder my pick with no colleague beside me. She goes adorned in a scarlet gown, with a big chain, and a banner and maces borne before her. Wouldn't Herbert be disgruntled at the sight? but I don't believe Vaughan would.

Shall I tell you my further plans? I come back in May, not having tried to earn a farthing meanwhile, because it is H. V. or die, this time. And by May I shall need to start in on one grind or another. The grind that attracts me most is digging in the blessed Bod. I am fairly good at it. And if by then you know of any Harvard don thirsting for historical or literary treasure-troves hidden in MSS., would you please recommend me as a diligent pig-headed miner?

There is a young cousin, Grace Guiney, likely to come live with me and be my love about that time; and I mean to set her digging too, but on genealogies and such things: she is a clever girl. I think of applying to the N. E. Genealogical Society for a commission. Don't you think it feasible? Not that I know any of our pundits there. But if they ever ran across my name, that might possibly be to Grace's advantage. She is very much like me in every way, only nicer and commits no po'try to speak of so far. . . .

You'll remember poor Tutin, the Yorkshire bookseller who is so fond of the old poets? He is just alive, and not much more, and is too weak to keep to his business. It is consumption.

I have had something to do lately with an edition of Lionel Johnson's prose papers, to be called, I think, *Post Liminium,* which Elkin Mathews will bring out about March. The editor is Prof. Whittemore of Tufts College, an old friend of mine, as was Lionel himself. It will be a sweet book, and worth while to have gathered, although most of it consists of unsigned reviews.

Goodnight. And soe fare well, hartilie commending you to God.

Yours ever,
L. I. GUINEY.

To Mary Winefride Day

OXFORD, *Dec. 14,* 1910.

MY DEAR POOR MARY,—I am so sorry I wrote yesterday, inquiring after little Dart, for the letter must have given you an extra pang. This morning I have a card from Preston, which sadly mentions your loss. So I must send you my love at once, and ever so loving a sympathy. I know too well what a thing it is to lose a creature from one's side who is all love. As Kipling says—

> "I have discovered how much I care,
> And have given my heart to a dog to tear."

Nothing can ever make me believe these little lives are thrown away and lost to us. Many saints say No: and Cornelius à Lapide, the great Jesuit commentator, bases on St. Paul, Rom. VIII, "the creature also," etc., a splendid statement for the immortality of animals. There should be one comfort for you besides, that Dart's little span was all sunshine, and of your own giving. Dear Mary, I am ever so sorry for you.

L. I. G.

To Bertram Dobell

71 MARLBOROUGH RD., FALMOUTH, *1 Feb.,* 1911.

DEAR MR. DOBELL,—This is so kind of you! I appreciate it. I will soon look carefully through the Catalogues, and return them. In a day or two I will do up your copy of Mrs. Willcox's *Manual,*[1] and send it home. I suppose Mr. Clarke told you he had shared it with me? and he instructed me to return it to you direct. It is, on the whole, a nice anthology: but I don't quite see what Mrs. Willcox's idea of Spiritual Fortification is, for the selections in some cases (*e. g.,* Donne's, Spenser's, Clough's) seem quite at random, and in others, she has managed to accumulate the most depressing, disheartening verses in the world!

This [2] about poor Hazlitt (a fool in nothing else, and he knew, as he says, that he "had elsewhere his inheritance") is abominably unkind. It would be impossible to write a review like that today: so we're not so bad as the Georgians, anyhow. I am not keeping it, though you kindly gave me the option, because I am not writing anything of late on W. H., and the cutting

[1] *A Manual of Spiritual Fortification,* being a choice of . . . poems, made by Louise Collier Willcox, 1910.

[2] A clipping from *John Bull,* 1823, concerning *Liber Amoris.*

might more safely lie among your papers than among mine, which (here at least) are in a tremendous state of confusion. I am up to the ears in Vaughan, this winter.

Every best wish, and many grateful thanks from

Yours sincerely always,

L. I. Guiney.

Oh, yes! Les Américaines are all pastured on English literature, more or less. They're Great Girls. Superb surf here, these days.

To Florence A. Crocker

71 Marlborough Rd., Falmouth, *Feb.,* 1911.

Thank you so much, Florence dear, for all your potent aid. I'll write the Bursar about the "mediæval nest," but if I have G. C. G. with me, how can we fit in? unless he has two mediæval nests! . . . I wish you would suggest to Mr. Powell something I have wished for many a year: *i.e.,* that Wellington Place should be re-named Chichele Place. This name would both connect it obviously with St. John's College, and prevent all confusion with horrid Wellington Square. I can't imagine the present Wellington Placers not welcoming the change for both reasons. Archbp. Chichele hasn't the smallest commemoration in the Oxford which owes so much to him.

I'm afraid you're overtaxing yourself about the word-hunting. All these definitions are immensely interesting, but if you would in future give me fewer examples,

&c., I should be happier for you. Tell Sir James Murray some day that Fulke Greville, Lord Brooke, uses "angel'd" (in *Mustapha,* Chorus Quintus Tartarorum) in the sense of "angelified":

> "So blest are they, so angel'd, so eternized;

and that Vaughan (in *Olor Iscanus,* To His Friend) uses it in a sense absolutely unique, so far as I can discover. He says of poets:

> "—angel'd from that sphere,
> By our strict guardians, (we're) kept luckless here."

What he has in mind is the exclusion from Paradise as detailed in Genesis, the angel with the flaming sword, &c., so that "angel'd" here means literally *policed;* driven out, kept out, by the celestial police-force. One reason why he is so hard to edit is that his text is full of individual usages like this, which has been made clear to me by your references copied from the blessed N. E. D. I'll be cruel cheerfully, however, and give you two more words, to be run down at your leisure. One is "revel." With this spelling, did it *ever* mean "reveille"? and was "reveil" ever an English word? and has it any meaning apart from the military one? If so, a couple of 17th cent. citations would be most welcome. Then—under "aprons," I suppose, "blew aprons": Vaughan again, apparently meaning the military guard at the Assizes, "bluecoats," as they were called later. I should so like to know the exact 17th cent. correlation of "blew aprons." Corbet's use of the word I know. . . .

A very tremendous wind was blowing all day yesterday, despite steady sunshine, and I never in all my life saw such surf as was rolling on Swanpool Beach. The breakers were not only prodigious (nothing but marine clotted cream as far as eye could see,—just a formless plunge and roar uniformly all over the surface) but the gale carried plumes and streamers of spray ten feet higher than each wave, and thirty feet further inland. Of course the road was covered, Swanpool itself drenched in salt spray, and those mighty stones you'll remember, the débris of the old sea-wall, were "swiggled" deep down into the sands. I never enjoyed anything more than that sight. I've watched rollers in many a storm, but this beat all. Coming home through Marlborough Road, I heard blackbirds in the hedges, a score of them; and the first splendid camelia tree was hung with its cherry-red flowers. Isn't that a true Cornish contrast? . . .

With thanks and love,

L. I. G.

To Strickland Gibson [1]

71 Marlborough Road, Falmouth, *3rd April,* 1911.

Dear Mr. Gibson,—I got greatly interested the other day, in an old Sotheby Sale Catalogue (1895) of a number of MSS. out of the famous Phillips Collec-

[1] Assistant librarian of the Bodleian Library, Oxford.

tion. I had no opportunity to copy page and number of the item which chiefly engaged my attention, a Household Book, XVI-XVIII centuries, having to do with the Nappers, and their descendants the Nevilles, once of Holywell Manor. Anyhow, it went to . . . the Right Place, *i. e.*, Bodley. I can hardly wait to get "home" to see it! Meanwhile, would it be of the slightest use by way of an extra item in the cataloguing, if I say that I think the "E. P." whose initials are said to be stamped upon the cover, can very easily be identified? Some time, at your leisure, just glance at a book published only two months ago, a big quarto, with illustrations, called *Forgotten Shrines,* and written by Dom Bede Camm, O. S. B. Pp. 149-182 comprise a chapter on the Catholic Napiers or Nappers of Holywell; by far the greater portion of it (barring the adjectives!) was of my own putting together, as you will see by the opening footnote. Well, I hardly think "E. P." can be any other than the Edmund Powell of Sandford mentioned on p. 177, whose sister married the "Oxford Martyr's" elder brother. He was much deferred to by all the Napier family. I take it for granted that the domestic chronicle mentioned at the bottom of p. 178 is not the MS. acquired by the Bodleian? but I really know nothing about it. Outside dear old Wood, there is no connected account in print of these very interesting people who lived at Holywell Manor, and I, for one, am delighted that the MS. is where it should have been long ago.

While we are talking of Bodley, may I congratulate

you on your gloriously good account of it?[1] I ran across it only last month: in spirit, in style, in workmanlike completion, in the big suggestive handling of a most difficult topic, nothing could possibly be better. "Sir, a gracefull Masterpeece!" My best wishes and remembrances, please, to Mr. Nicholson.

Yours always,
L. I. GUINEY.

To Bertram Dobell[2]

April 28th, 1911.

I don't think I expressed myself well in regard to your "theology": it is only the negations I fall foul of: on the constructive side you are, and seem to me, absolutely sound, though, as an excellent critic once said of Hazlitt, you "praise the right things for the wrong reasons"! and I can see that your case has been that of many another truth-loving and honourable soul: you have been repelled by the distortion, narrowness, and spiritual smugness, not of Christianity, but of the adjacent descant upon it: *i. e.,* Evangelical Protestantism. Hence what you think is your atheism: I call it nothing of the sort, but a very high-minded religion of a kind, floundering through a darkness and loneliness which need not be. These remarks are no part of my criticism, but I thought you would take them in good part from an out-and-out Catholic.

---

[1] "Oxford Libraries," an article in *Book-Auction Records,* vol. 8, pt. 1 (1911). This was afterwards enlarged and published as *Some Oxford Libraries,* Oxford University Press, 1914.

[2] Postscript from a letter criticising Mr. Dobell's poems.

To E. W. B. Nicholson

71 MARLBORO' ROAD, FALMOUTH, *April 29*, 1911.

DEAR MR. NICHOLSON,—I make bold to send you a roll of *Academies*, containing an unnecessarily split-up paper of mine, a very dry-as-dust affair, indeed, annotating a secular poem of Vaughan's. Of course the Oxford water-mark, which I think I see in every line of it, is my excuse for commending it to you at all. . . . The thing provided me with some fun in the writing, but I don't know whether I have made it really conclusive.

Aren't you quite built up again? I shall be disappointed when I get back, to hear any other news. Suppose you let me send you some Cornish clotted cream, by way of magic potion? Will you? That would give me particular pleasure; and it couldn't harm Your Bookship?

Sincerely yours
L. I. GUINEY.

To Herbert E. Clarke, Esq.

OXFORD, *June 29*, 1911.

Wie gehts, Sire of the Teutonick Fellow?[1] There is nobody to beat you for flashes of silence; and you never write unless you're written to, do you? Didst coronate? My "niece,"—they *will* call her that,—and I passed the day in a Berkshire field, with many cherries and a book or two. Since when, as before, we have

[1] Francis Clarke, Fellow of All Souls; Oxford.

been house-hunting. I think I have found the thing we want, very near the old abode on Winchester Road which does not enshrine all sweetest memories. I shall decide ere long, and you shall hear. I can't do a bit of scribble until my own belongings are again about me. Nor have I found as yet a single free half-day for the *isola beata Bodleiana*. Letters and people and small affairs make up, after all, the worst sort of a life. Mr. Carew Hazlitt and his daughter are here, in picturesque rooms I found for them: I hadn't seen either since 1895! but that seems hardly so long ago as last week. I have been presented with the new large book called *The Hazlitts,* privately printed. It has its uses, but it isn't W. H. In July I am to join one long-loved Agnes Evans of Yarnton on a unique lark involving a fortnight's residence in a barge drawn by a gee-gee along the Berks and Wilts canal. Will you and Agnes come too? Simple but nutritious; plenty of rain promised, especially by night; cleanliness rather at a discount, etc., etc. They are making a deck for us. Total sharable costs, 22s per week. Wouldn't it be good for you to join the aquatic mixed monastery? Mrs. Evans has been wanting to hire a barge for years, and now she has done it. She and her lord are great local antiquaries and topographers.

Oh, the pendulum weather! We roast, we freeze. Please let me know how you are. I wish I knew, and think thoughts when I don't. *Vivite, valete,* ye distant and dumb! with old love,

L. I. G.

To The Rev. J. J. Burke, C. S. P.

OXFORD, *9 July,* 1911.

DEAR FR. BURKE,—I owe you thanks for your good intention of making me acquainted with your brother, and I do hope I shall not miss him. Just now, I am in the egregiously uncomfortable position of having no address! as I am soon to leave these lodgings, and shall not have our little house until the middle of August, if I can only capture the one I want. And meanwhile, from July 20th until August 11th or so, I am off gypsying, far from post-offices and railroads, with my young cousin and our friend Mrs. Evans, who loves, like myself, to lapse now and then into complete anonymity and *il*locality. But I should not relish missing Fr. Burke, as I began by saying!

Now I should love to write that paper which you suggest to me. But I clearly can't! I can guess pretty closely, I think, at the sort of thing you want, approving the catalogue movement in the main, but endeavouring to guide it along sound critical and above all, soundly Catholic-spirited lines. I am off the ground, dear Father, and not in touch with the thing; and then these lists are mostly fiction, and I never read fiction if I can help it, and am no judge of it when I do. The only remark, even, which I could make upon the subject, would be that it is a fallacy to suppose Catholic authors must produce what can truthfully be described as Catholic books. Of course some must, and do, bless them! But the general premise simply doesn't exist, and no logical deduction can be made until it does. Besides, you know my fixed theory which really you will say

I have sufficiently "aired" already: that American so-so Catholics have everything to learn of English through-and-through Catholics. Would you care to ask Fr. Havens Richards, S. J., to do that paper, authoritatively? The subject is his hobby. If I knew one fiftieth as much about it as he does, I shouldn't dream of refusing. Anyhow, I thank you ever so much for asking me. I hope you may like *Lovelace and Vaughan.*

Yours ever, dear Father,
L. I. GUINEY.

To Dr. Henry Bradley [1]

117 WOODSTOCK RD., OXFORD, *28 Nov.,* 1911.

MY DEAR DR. BRADLEY,—I never go "much of anywhere," but I have been following in print your fascinating lecture on local place-names. Like many other folk, I find some of my cherished notions (or ignorances) knocked on the head.

I wish Mrs. Bradley and Miss Ellie would ask me up to tea (!) soon, that you may demolish them [2] and me. Meanwhile, while preparing to run away quick, I just dare to utter this much: if Oxenford means the ox-ford, how are we to get around the fact, if it be a fact, that the Saxons herded only sheep and swine? And then Fritwell as the "divining well,"—I wonder if you would possibly think the theory holds water that Fritwell might be Frithuswith's Well, as Epwell is Eppa's Well? I have one and a half very special

[1] The distinguished philologist, chief editor, after Sir James Murray's death, of the *New English Dictionary.* He died in May, 1923.
[2] Not the FAMILY, but the IGNORANCES. [L. I. G.]

reasons for thinking this, which no one has so far brought into play: and I got them from old MS. Latin Lives of S. Frideswide. Oh, dear! hear me saying my say to Plato himself, as it were . . . the bragian 'ussy that is

Your ever devoted
L. I. GUINEY.

To Dr. Henry Bradley

117 WOODSTOCK RD., OXFORD, *28 Nov.*, 1911

MY DEAR DR. BRADLEY,—I treasure your letter, and am most eager to be converted. I wish I had my reference (I haven't anything that is mine hereabouts) about the "herding" of oxen among the Saxons. It was not an old one. I gathered that it meant, not indeed that they possessed no oxen in farmstead byres, or on monastic lands, but that their number was very limited, and that they were not turned out to graze in fields and woods, by the score or hundred, as sheep and swine were, with their separate stockades and herdsmen. However, I am more than willing, as I began by saying, to get at the "fact"! Also, if Oxford is Oxenaford, the worthy ox of the city shield and of the Frideswide in Wolsey's *Evangelisterium*, is not so unhistoric as he has been thought to be! Thank you.

"Fritwell" is a more complicated business. No, I haven't one scrap of evidence to show that any mediæval chronicler ever dreamed of it as formerly Frituswitewylla. I am the only mediæval chronicler who did! You see all the oldest (12th cent.) hagiologists say she fled away to "Bentona," which the 14th and 15th century writers translate as they please, Abingdon, Benson, Bampton, and Binsey. The oldest MSS. also state that she lived in a swineherd's hut in a wood not very far from Bentona: and that the well was discovered there (*in sylvam*) in answer to her prayer. Now my bold geographical guess is that Bentona is Bainton, sometimes spelled Beanton, at present a mere hamlet in Stoke Lyne parish, ("Stoke" is itself a minor argument, is it not?) and that Frithuswith's Well may be at Fritwell, between three and four miles away from the "ton." Fritwell Church belongs to Christ Church; the much discussed carving on the tympanum, with its symbolical tree and the attendant wild boars, harmonises well with her legend. It all seems to me a hazardous, but by no means crazy guess. No one of the other presumable "Bentonas," except Bampton, ever stood in a forest tract, and none of them ever had any ancient connection with Ch. Ch. This is putting it baldly, and trying to cover ground with a sentence or two. The least disproof would make me abandon Frituswitewylla. But my game is to wait for it. I am not publishing my precious theory! Fritwell Well is a shabby pump in the road near the Church, and Binsey Well (an absolute impostor!) has the inscription and the historical or myth-loving pilgrims.

I do hope Mrs. Bradley is better. She has more than her share, poor dear. My love to her. Yours ever,

L. I. GUINEY.

To Dr. Henry Bradley

117 WOODSTOCK RD., *Nov. 30,* 1911.

DEAR DR. BRADLEY,—You comfort me greatly by thinking that my Bentona-Fritwell theory may be a good working hypothesis. Did I ever say that the name Frithuswith appears under rather odd forms in the old MSS.? Fredwid, Friswith, Frewisse (!) are among these. "Fretewelle" might have some conceivable connection with the first of them; but no guess of mine can get around the "Fertewelle" with which also I am pretty familiar. I forgot to remark that the dedication of Fritwell Church is to S. Olaf, while the tympanum of the porch, the north door, the stoup, etc., are Saxon work, and much older than King Olaf's time. There must, therefore, have been a church formerly there, under another dedication. Now, just suppose for a moment that this dedication was to S. Frideswide, or that the place was connected with her history and tradition. Well, a big Danish settlement sprang up in those parts (witness Dun's Tew, just across the Cherwell); and Oxfordshire Danes must have hated the name Frideswide like poison, since the great massacre in 1002, (or was it 1004 A. D.?) in our Ch. Ch., always then called S. Frideswide's. So they may have proceeded "with great gusto and éclat" to rededicate her Church in Fritwell to their national hero. Nothing would be more natural; and this upside-downing, supposing that it did occur, might quite well explain, might it not, the entire absence of a local tradition of the Saxon Abbess? After all, seven hundred years, (from the substitution of S. Olaf,) is a long time, and even an English village's memory has been known to lapse in less. Could the derivation of Fritwell ever be proved to link itself with Frithuswith, why, that name it bears would imply a tradition indeed.

On the whole, I am pleased as Punch and proud as a peacock that I had your leave, as it were, to keep the taper of my pet hobby burning. (I will see it blown out, if needs be, by facts, without turning a hair.) Ever so many thanks to you for this pleasant correspondence. Believe me, dear Dr. Bradley, yours ever,

L. I. GUINEY.

To Strickland Gibson

LONGWALL COTTAGE, OXFORD, *26th March,* 1912.

DEAR MR. GIBSON,—This is nothing to answer. I only wanted to tell you that I have sent a few paragraphs to the *Oxford Times* (to be in print, I suppose, this coming Friday) about Mr. Nicholson; I should like *your* eye to see it there. I hope it shows no undue heat, but it is astonishing to me to hear such remarks about him as I have lately heard from several North Oxford quarters, and I could but do my best to thwart them. I can't bear it, this stupidity which finds petty faults in so large-souled a man. As you imagine, Bodley won't seem the same place to me. I really loved him much. You have all my sympathy in the loss of so good a friend.

Yours ever sincerely,
L. I. GUINEY.

No. Cerney, near Cirencester,
Easter Tuesday [*9 April*], 1912.

To Mary Winefride Day

You dear Mary Day,—Your letter has reached me here, where I am staying alone for a few days' rest, in bracing hilly air, and most glorious Easter sunshine. I was so glad to hear from you, and to realize that you are so brave and calm under such a keen loss. That such young souls stay at all in this world is one of the best arguments I know for the blessed hereafter: for they are here, so to speak, prepaid for a return to their native land, and are obviously (as most of us are not) *concives angelorum*. You are happy to have had your little Mary, and to be sure of having her again.

And now, how can I thank you for such a big fine gift? Imagine your thinking of me and my cottage at all, with so much on your mind! I do appreciate it, and thank you with all my heart. Some day you must come and see our secluded abode. In it there will certainly be two big candlesticks, and a plebeian but much-desired TUB, which are not there now: thanks to you. This latter (a most superior object!) for *my* girl's room. She is the cheeriest creature, and is now able to take quite long walks. I am getting her out here on Friday, and we go back to Oxford together, on foot part of the way, unless new floods intercept us. . . . I heard my Easter Mass at Cirencester, where we have a sweet little new Church. Also, such a superb old Parish Church that it rouses all sorts of greeds and resentments!

Love to you, dearest Mary. Keep well, and let me hear from you when you can and will.

Yours always,
L. I. GUINEY.

To The Rev. J. J. Burke, C. S. P.

LONGWALL COTTAGE, OXFORD, *19 April*, 1912.

DEAR FR. BURKE,—What must you think of me? I never responded to your request about *Ethan Frome*, and never even thanked you for the gift of the book! Do forgive me. I haven't any real excuse except that I haven't been particularly well all winter (a misbehaving heart is the matter) and seem to have shirked many things on that account. But I wasn't as much struck with the workmanship of Mrs. Wharton's grim tale as your correspondent was, who so kindly wished to see my criticism of it in print. And as for its complete Godlessness, I didn't quite see why Mrs. Wharton should be made a scapegoat for that, the most terrible characteristic of modern New England fiction. Mrs. Wilkins Freeman is a great exponent of it, perhaps especially in *Pembroke;* so is Hamlin Garland, so is Arlo Bates, and in some degree, even my own friend Alice Brown. God, and the moral law, and the barrier of conscience, when it comes to a crisis, do not exist for our novelists: but that is no special reason for whacking *Ethan Frome:* and I hadn't the necessary knowledge (being out of the contemporary stream these last years) to treat the subject in a comprehensive way: hence I wrote nothing upon it. You were more than good to send the book. I have to thank you, too, for my copy, and Miss Johnson's copy, of the new *C. W.*, with Lionel's Gibbon paper. The verse dedicated to his memory by Edward O'Brien comes from a very interesting Boston lad: do you know him? He has much in him, if he doesn't get spoiled, and in looks he is the image of Lionel's self.

Two days ago I wrote a longish review, on a precious little book, Digby Dolben's poems, which appeal directly to a Catholic public, though not published for them. I mean to copy it out and send it to you. If you like it well enough to print it, may I claim a privilege you once proffered me, and ask to have it paid for on acceptance? and also to have the pennies,—whatever they are,—involved in my long-since-accepted "Lovelace and Vaughan"? I shall be grateful. This news of the *Titanic* has darkened everything. Please remember me most amicably to M. l'Abbé *votre frère.*

Yours ever, dear Father,

L. I. GUINEY.

To The Rev. J. J. Burke, C. S. P.

LONGWALL COTTAGE, OXFORD, *2 July,* 1912.

MY DEAR FR. BURKE,—It rejoices me that you "take" to my dear boy Digby Dolben. I had known some of his verses for a dozen years, but never hoped to see them gathered together. The book here costs 10/6. The present copyright seems to belong to Mr. Bridges himself, and he seems hard to deal with: I know he is hemming and hawing and keeping on tenterhooks his own friend Mr. Orby Shipley, who wants some of the verses for his new *Lyra Eucharistica;* so I dare say he would say No at once to any transatlantic request. But would this not solve part of your difficulty, if I posted my copy to you? In fact, I am doing so, and you need not return the darling thing until I get back to this house in September. What is to prevent your getting the little hymns for the children typewritten and taught at St. Paul's? That is not publishing them; and you will need no permission, legal or moral, to put that through. They are really touching. Miss Dolben, Digby's only sister, and the last of the family, died aged about seventy-seven a few months ago, at Finedon Hall. A cousin (of course non-Catholic) has since come into possession, I hear, of the estate.

A thousand thanks for the delightful book of the Stations. How very kind of you to send it to me! I shall value it and its inscription. About the Newman articles. No subject could be more tempting. Alas, I cannot face any new work, not even a short paper, for a long time to come. All my planned work is so desperately in arrears. I haven't been very well; and *avalanches* (nothing less!) of American friends and acquaintances have thrown themselves across my accustomed tracks. No fewer than fifteen here yesterday! How would it do to ask Fr. McNabb to write you such a Newman analysis and defence as you want? He would do it, if he has time, infinitely better than I could. The address is: The Very Rev. Vincent McNabb, O. P., Holy Cross Priory, Leicester, England. He is Prior there. Do you know him? A spirit; ardent, youngish, full of fire and genius. With thanks and affection,

L. I. GUINEY.

Thank you also for my copy and Miss I. Johnson's of *C. W.* What a wrong-headed, silly, and cruel attack on Lionel in *America* of June 15th.

To Agnes G. Evans [1]

HELMSLEY, YORKS, *July,* 1912.

DEAREST Ζωη,—Your good little letter was welcomed hotly—and in such hot weather, too! You would love it here, only the walking is so inevitable, and so rough. Heavenly dales and villages, and wonderfully romantic bits of history, and the very best people in all England. My landlady is a "sample"; a miracle of cleanliness, of cookery, and of generosity: keeps a plate always piled with gooseberries and raspberries, between meals, in the room; and flowers, too, abound daily. One guinea a week, mind you, and chicken *thrice* since I came! We can't afford fowl at home. It took me many days to get rested and "keyed up," but now I am in great form, scribbling away like mad, and hoping to get no fewer than six pot-boilers done, before I turn homeward. Dear me, how I love

[1] Mrs. Herbert A. Evans, an enthusiastic local antiquary, wrote for the *Oxford Times,* over several years, a weekly column called the Zodiac and signed Ζωη. These articles attracted L. I. G.'s attention and led to a lasting friendship with their writer and her husband, who was the author of *Highways and Byways in Oxford and the Cotswolds.*

freedom and solitude! They expand me "powers" as nothing else can. . . .

As usual, I read your *Zodiac* with great attention. Such a nice account of St. Michael's: so few ever mention, or notice, for that matter, that little variant of the *danse macabre*. I suppose you will describe the old glass in north aisle? I love that, but don't see how it can be an Annunciation, despite the poetical lily, flowering forth a Calvary. The left-hand figure next Our Lady might be Elizabeth, don't you think? and the outer elderly one on the right hand a St. Anne? the whole a Visitation? The old *chancel* glass I think ugly, but I suppose it is precious. You didn't say that your friend Dionysia Burewald lived, and the Burewald ancestors lived, in that dear stone-gabled house opposite St. Michael's, which has just been sliced away so cruelly; nor that Ship St. once bore their name. These poor chantrey folk in the Middle Ages, with their pathetic bequests "for ever". . .!

I am going to send you a dear little brass knocker for your Ship St. door. It is only 1s 6d, so don't scold! It comes from that man in Ripon, a real mediæval artist, who copies old work so skilfully. I have just heard of a said-to-be-lovely old cottage, furnished, at Hinton Marvel near Wimborne, cupboards, garden (big) and what not, plus a thatch, for 10s a week in winter: six rooms. You and I must start that agency some day!

With love ever,

L. I. G.

To Bertram Dobell

CROPREDY, *Jan. 3*, 1913.

DEAR MR. DOBELL,—The best of all New Years to you! It will be a nice one for many of us if you publish your *Gleanings from Manuscripts* before it passes. You can imagine how intensely interested I was in what you say of "Mr. Barnard" on "Mrs. Jernagan." (This, I suppose, is one of the Jerninghams? a prominent family, easily traced. And the 17th century parish registers at Acton, as I happen to know, are extant, and legible.) I vehemently love and adore *The Exequy*: but as you truly say, King never touched that high-water mark elsewhere. I cannot but think it addressed to a dead wife. I did not know anything of Mrs. King except that she existed, and died young; but knowing that beloved age as I may say I do, I agree with you, up to the point of uttermost emphasis, that it would have been impossible, were there five King children, that no mention of them should occur in the poem. Rather, there would have been too much mention: and at least a dozen "conceits" playing around it. But who, oh, who, was "Mr. Barnard"? There is a quite wonderfully beautiful anonymous "exequy" in *Melpomene, or The Muses' Delight,* printed in 1678. I have often pondered over it: it belongs, surely, to the preceding generation. Nobody but Rochester could have written it, after 1660; and I am confident that Rochester didn't! That dustheap genius was capable of the very most angel-like lyric notes. I wish you would unriddle that authorship, too. As someone said of Opie, you are such a fine mouser.

The Bazaar gave me much pleasure, and I thank you for it. I like little in it better than your gay Hibernicism: I remembered it well. The Oxford University Press folk gave me a copy of "Q's" admirable anthology.[1] Mine own contributions are most queerly printed: lines broken up, and words altered, almost as if Sir Arthur had done me the extraordinary compliment of dictating them from memory! The metrical lapses and irregularities you complain of in my peasant's song, are of malice prepense: to convey the idea of a sob here and there: but perhaps they don't succeed in doing it? . . . I have been up here in a quiet cottage for a few days, trying to sleep, and not scoring a very brilliant success. I return to-morrow.

Yours ever,
L. I. GUINEY.

To Clement Shorter

LONGWALL COTTAGE, OXFORD, *Jan. 22,* 1913.

MY DEAR MR. SHORTER,—What a big pleasure you have given me, in sending me Dora's book! I love her wild direct art, as you know, and the opening poem, the Prayer (one of the two here which I had never seen before), quite took my breath away with its elemental truth and sadness. If Dora would only keep a colon, a pet dearer to me, or to Lionel Johnson once, than to anybody "since Charles was King," her lines would hit every thoughtful reader, for ever, between the eyes! Thank you ever so much. And for the

---

[1] *The Oxford Book of Victorian Verse,* edited by Sir Arthurs Quiller-Couch.

tickets, too. You shall have the paragraph, and promptly. They are fine seats for a "deafy" like me. Now, in regard to the rest of your letter, I am going to tell you frankly that you hurt me very much, and I do not think you meant to do that. Nor do I know why you should recur to the thought of me whenever fickleness is attributed (why?) to us Americans; for I am entirely incapable of going back on old friends. I want you, and Dora too, to be gentle with me. You are free folk, happy in being able to work out your ideals to write, to move about, to keep in touch with life and art. I have gone for the last six years from one disappointment and heartbreak to another; I have been thwarted in every single thing I hoped to do; and I have as small a stock of nervous strength to bluff it with as anyone I know. When you talk of my "careering about England," do you realize that I never go away at all except when I am dead fagged, or when, to get the merest pot-boiler done, I must escape from interruptive Oxford? that I visit no friend's house, but go into humble lodgings where I live for months on end, absolutely alone? If you did, you could hardly reproach me for not having set foot in London but once in the last three years (except for my dear Herbert Clarke's burial),[1] and then it was because I was ill, and had to go to a specialist. As to my getting "offended," what nonsense! I am guiltless of that, so far, in my career. The gate wouldn't open to me, the last time; but what of that? I should have tried it again, when the chance came. After all, I have always sent a greeting at

[1] In January, 1912.

Christmas, even this year, when I hadn't the grit for such things, for the most part, and do you think I make it a grudge that you have not done the same thing? Oh, no. As I began by saying, I cannot change towards those who have been so kind to me, in my happier days. I would send you a poem even without asking, if only I had one. My Muse is a jade, and never turns up while there is a cloudlet in the sky. I sent the *Windsor* an old verse, which had never been offered to anyone. It was topographical, and evidently appealed to Mr. Hutchinson. Goodbye, and my love to Dora, at the end of a confessional script not very typical of

Yours as ever,

L. I. GUINEY.

To Bertram Dobell

LONGWALL COTTAGE, OXFORD, *Jan. 29,* 1913.

DEAR MR. DOBELL,—This makes a most interesting article: do print it. I don't think it proves much, however, for "Mr. Barnard." On thinking things over, I take back my saying (in agreement with your theory) that mention of the children, etc., would have been almost inevitable had the Bishop's young wife been the subject of *The Exequy.* Vaughan lost his first wife Katharine Wise about 1653; she, too, was very young, and left four infants behind. I am convinced, being, as you know, an old student of H. V., that he quite plainly alludes to her in some four poems, and to her throughout in two: yet nowhere is there the smallest biographical specification. Perhaps King was of that same very reticent and fugitive sensitiveness. It was not, and is not, common.

How direct and "masculine" is the Lady Anne,[1] and how hard she can hit! In a certain homespun and underived felicity of phrase, especially of metaphor, she reminds me of Orinda, and also of Ephelia. Do you know Ephelia? Such a fine old girl! I haven't the least idea who she was. When next I get to Bodley, I am going to look up "Sweating cradles" for you, and see whether R. Compton's *Mansion of Magnanimity* is in the Catalogue. Meanwhile, very best thanks for this nice loan.

Yours ever,
L. I. Guiney.

To Rev. Henry Shandelle, S. J., Georgetown College, Washington, D. C.

Longwall Cottage, Oxford, *June 18,* 1913.

Dear Fr. Shandelle,—I have such a funny request to make of you: for you are the one I naturally write to. You know I am anything but notional, and surely not given to interfering? Yet I am going to beg you to ask something of Fr. Provincial. My own name would count for nothing in the matter; I have no stake in it, nothing to lose or gain. It is just an impersonal and abstract request. So here goes—A. M. D. G.!

I have within a month been looking over some old *Americas*. It strikes me for the hundredth time, but strikes me much harder than ever before, what an ex-

[1] Countess of Dorset, Pe oroke and Montgomery.

traordinary literary talent is Fr.———'s. For pure belle-lettristic criticism he is above any English-speaking man in the Society: and I am not forgetting, in saying so, four or five over here, "whose praise is in all the Churches." He has fallen silent of late, which is a pity. I never saw him; we exchanged two letters once, long ago, and that is all I know about him, except that he is teaching somewhere out West. Now would the idea commend itself (and if *you* suggested it, I can not but believe it would) to Fr. Provincial to send Fr. ——— to England for at least a year? to be in London, or Stonyhurst, or Bournemouth, or Beaumont, or,—best of all, perhaps, Oxford,—or anywhere where the Society has a house, where he would not be called upon for much work beyond the very beautiful work he would have leisure to do? I am sure he would look upon the opportunity as a godsend; and I am sure the atmosphere of the Old World would ripen his genius (it is nothing short of genius of the sympathetic and interpretative kind) in a wonderful way. I have no idea what may be Fr.———'s age: but it doesn't matter, as souls have none.

I am actuated in writing all this, by, I suppose, a sort of clannishness. I do so rejoice in good work, and get so wearied at all the bother made (at least in our country) over work which is third-rate. And, as an equally strong second motive, I am jealous for the Society, and want all its ammunition put to the best possible use. Hence my strong impression in regard to Fr. ———, and the persistent wish, yes, and prayer, that the Fr. Provincial might pin a pair of wings on his shoulders. They would be dedicated wings, not singe-able by this world's candle-flames. Do get him that much liberty! If Mr. Rockwell be still Fr. Provincial's secretary, you might commend to him also my scheme *pro fide et patria,* and let him help to bring it before Fr. Provincial in due form and season. I take it that the Society's changings about, at home as here, occur at midsummer? If the air of the great Catholic past, and the touch of it, like deep moss under one's feet in a wood, doesn't bring some most cherishable books out of Fr. ———s' kind of mind, I should be hanged for a no-prophet! What on earth *he* would think of me for thus pondering his future fate, I know not. But I have had the thing steadily in mind for some time. I believe it must turn out the right thing, once it gets Fr. Provincial's sanction. And there I leave it. . . .

I hope you keep well, dear Fr. Shandelle, and that the Library has had all its burns healed? As for me, I am always well enough and happy enough, but just a bit too busy. Two delightful young cousins, orphans, Grace and Ruth Guiney (21 and 16), my only relatives, have come over here to live with me. The latter is at the Holy Child Convent School at Mayfield, and both are Catholicizing at a great rate! but not de-Americanizing, I am glad to say. . . . Grace has the Guiney turn for scribbling,—if I can only make her see that there is no art without toil! She has a very pleasant secretarial post nine miles from Oxford. Add a dog and a cat (both the most idiosyncratic of beasties), and you will see that I have about as many family cares as my old age will require. Pray for

Yours ever affectionately,
LOUISE I. GUINEY.

To Clement Shorter

LONGWALL COTTAGE, OXFORD, *Aug. 11,* 1913.

DEAR MR. SHORTER,—Thank you so much. If it be not already in print, will you give me my commas and colons? Also, be a Dear, and knock off "well-known" before my luckless name. I once wrote an essaylet "On being Well-known." The adjective is this bull's special red rag! I should like it better if you would just say: "An Oxford correspondent sends us the following appreciation."

Yours always,
L. I. G.

To Miss Warner

LONGWALL COTTAGE, OXFORD, *2 September,* 1913.

DEAR MISS WARNER,—Your letter of inquiry has just come. Being a lover of Vaughan, I should rejoice to have you do him honour, did I not honestly think he is by now a subject not fresh enough for such a thesis as you speak of. Even the study of his way of treating Nature, and the comparison between him and Wordsworth, or between him and Blake, has been made, and well made. If you like seventeenth-century subjects, I can perhaps suggest a few quite unhackneyed ones (not all literary) for which there is abundant manuscript material over here. I might name, rather at random:

1. Anne, Countess of Dorset, Pembroke, and Montgomery: friend of many poets, builder of castles, etc., all over the North: a most interesting woman.

2. Fairfax the Parliamentary leader: Fairfax *fils*. There's a fragrant old MS. volume of his "private meditations," etc.—which nobody knows, in the Bodleian.

3. Constable: (a bit earlier in point of time) Quarles: Wither: Denham. These poets are all practically unedited. The third one's voluminousness, however, might prove disconcerting.

4. A poetess known as "Ephelia." Too slight a clue, perhaps, to lead one to identifying her. Her book of verses is in print, and is as good as "Orinda's."

5. The Treatment of The Child in English Poetry. Is that a subject you would care to handle historically? Blake and Wordsworth would play up here, as well as Vaughan, Traherne, and countless lesser fry of the old days.

6. Henry More the Cambridge Platonist and his friends the Conways. There is a whole unpublished set of letters in the Br. Museum, if I mistake not, passing between them, which should make most delightful reading. Poet, Philosopher, and academician. More is a man of genius not yet generally known. I don't know whether any of these will attract you. My Vaughan work (I mean to do it with a colleague, whose charge is the biographical part) is very much hung up

at present. I can't get the unbroken leisure such a big task needs.

Accept my best wishes for your success, and believe me

Sincerely yours,
L. I. GUINEY.

To Clement Shorter

LONGWALL COTTAGE, OXFORD, *9 Jan.,* 1914.

DEAR MR. SHORTER,—I am sure it was you (I'd almost rather say I'm sure it was dear old Dora!) who sent me the book for a Christmas gift? A very delightful book it is, spontaneous and forthright, like all D.'s work, and full of quality; quite up to her very best, some of these short things are. I do rejoice in such a maintained artistry. And it almost makes me wish I knew how to envy it! because envy is such a true compliment, and should be paid here if anywhere. My own Muse won't waggle a tail-feather, not for years past, and the leisure for reading and writing never comes. My love to Dora, and the Happiest of New Years be hers from—Someone Else.

Miss Pringle is still twittering with the pleasure your little letter about her *Sphere* poem gave her. She even timorously inquires whether I think she might some time submit another one to you? She is a dear.

Did you ever get time to look at the anthology I sent you?[1] It seems an interesting sheaf to me, though I deprecate the inclusion of Le Gallienne as an "Amer-

[1] *The Little Book of Modern American Verse,* edited by Jessie Rittenhouse.

ican"; and could spare, without weeping, at least three rather pompous and Marmorean self-conscious geniuses among the men. But some of the women are ever so good, to atone. My own lyrics seem mostly of the sticky-sweet sort, not very characteristic, I do hope. The compiler is no mean critic. It should be "A Little Book, &c.," not "The Little Book, &c." Some of my favourite moderns, most original but not widely known, are unluckily left out, and not tons of Le Gallienne can fill the gap. Best wishes and Goodnight.

"Yours am I, though I seem not,
And will be, though I show not."—(SIDNEY?)

L. I. GUINEY.

To Helen Ellis

LONGWALL COTTAGE, OXFORD, *15 Aug.,* 1914.

MY DEAR MISS ELLIS,—We never hear from you! so I am sending some just-plucked lavender to remind you and Miss Appleton (to whom my love and half of the few sprays) of Longwall Cottage. Just now it is floating my huge old Auburndale Stars and Stripes, flanked by two Union Jacks. We had a meeting here yesterday of Americans in Oxford (residents and tourists), to see what we could do to help our gallant England in this crisis. The spirit of the public is altogether admirable; one doesn't know how sufficiently to admire the self-control and self-sacrifice on all sides. It is the most quietly heroic thing ever seen: something, I fancy, that must have been known before, in our Civil War, fought, like this dreadful one now breaking, on a moral issue. So many dear boys I know have gone or are going! They say there will be no October Term. The High is full of soldiers and nurses, and the Red Cross folk, as if by magic, have turned the Masonic Hall buildings, and the great Examination Schools opposite to them (both at our very gate) into immense fully-equipped hospitals: all awaiting, and providing for, horrors to come. . . . I do hope Kaiserism will get its lasting quietus: the world will be a far more decent place without it. . . .

To Agnes Purday

LONGWALL COTTAGE, OXFORD, *31 Aug.*, 1914.

DEAREST AGNES,—You don't write, and I keep wondering how the war is affecting you [in Austria]. Did you get my last, with the lavender? Things are at a great pitch of excitement these days, although all is outwardly quiet enough. They say the first British wounded arrived to-day at our great Red Cross hospital over the way, the Examination Schools. We Americans over here are each and every one well in for it, and in divers ways at the disposal of the Emergency Committee. Ruth has been called upon already as Messenger, Usher at a meeting, Flower-seller in the streets for the Relief Fund (the young folk, in one rainy afternoon, took over £52) and Sewer-in-ordinary for Belgian refugees. Besides that, she is learning First Aid. Poor kiddie! She can't get to Tournai now. I can't even get an answer from her Convent. This means a lot to us both. I doubt if even by January poor little broken Belgium will be a safe place for a young girl to cross alone. I have had two other disappointments directly due to the war. The net result is that after a careful survey of the situation on all sides, I find I must give up this nice dear house. I have the option of breaking the lease at Michaelmas (3 yrs. here) and should have to clear out before Christmas. I dread it beyond everything: the upset, the loss of my admirable and devoted Annie, &c., and most of all, the consignment of your goods and treasures to the warehouse again. . . . Now, dear Agnes, don't take this to heart for my sake, after your unselfish fashion, and begin propounding ways to help, &c. I have made up my mind I am unhelpable. Ill luck simply loves me and dogs me, and I am now quite used to it; and if after constant work and the denial of just about every pleasure I can't *both* pay my bills and live in peace,—why, I will do the former every time, and trust Providence that I may somehow land on my feet when I have jumped into vacancy. I haven't had time to think out what I shall do next: whether just lodge in some far-off quiet spot, or be bolder, and take a cottage in the country. I suppose the former would be the lesser risk, at least for the present. . . .

I do so hope you are absolutely safe and well. So many dear boys I know have gone to the front. It is a most heart-rending business for the Allies to have to fight such a conscienceless foe as Germany has shown herself to be. I don't say "brutal," because that is too disrespectful to the brutes. Were it not for the Fleet, what is to prevent those murderers from sacking London and Oxford? God save England and the righteous cause! . . .

With much affection, yours ever,

LOUISE.

To Helen Ellis

Feb. 1, 1915.

. . . Your letter was wonderfully welcome, and quite warmed my heart. There was no war then! . . . It is hard to keep one's daily rounds unperturbed, with the German "frightfulness" likely to burst at any moment over the adored spires of Oxford. A bomb on the Bodleian,—and certainly my life, for one, would be worth little thereafter. . . . Talk about "neutrality" and about "peace" makes one sick. As if one could be neutral while an abominable miscreant oligarchy is seeking to devour Europe, or wish to make peace with a dragon until his skin is hung up to dry! I am glad to be here, whatever dangers may be here too, for it is one of England's great hours, and we shall see her, or what is left of her, crowned. The refugee Belgians (eight hundred of them in little Oxford, including many Louvain professors, and more are to come) are admirable folk for courage and patience; and for silence, too. Everybody tends and shields and venerates them, in a way beautiful to see. Each village has its well-looked-after "guests." I am writing from Adderbury, near Banbury: do you know this sweet place? I have just got well after a month's illness, so shall go home soon. As I came out to recuperate, and could neither read nor write, but wanted some live interest, I brought along with me a friend's collie who was in ever so bad a way. You know I am an experienced vet.! So Cym is now, dear fellow, as fit as a fiddle and as handsome as a lord. . . .

To A. K. Gibson, of Grand Rapids, Michigan

LONGWALL COTTAGE, OXFORD, *April 28,* 1915.

DEAR MR. GIBSON,—Your query should have been answered before, but I have been away, and ill, and, after that, overwhelmed with things to do. The little Catholic essays of Lionel's, which Fr. Burke printed, were the shavings, so to speak, of *Post Liminium:* rejected from that general collection not in the least because their quality wasn't just as high, but only because they had a special intimate note of religiousness, or else were skirmishes more or less along the same line as some longer papers used in the book. They came from many sources, mostly from London weeklies, and none were in MS. when sent to New York. I am so glad you treasure not only the gold, but the gold dust of L. J.

Mr. Elkin Mathews isn't so much to blame, I suppose, for the delays, as the unconscionable Mr. [Arthur] Galton, who never should have been accepted as the author-to-be of the Memoir. I lent him all the letters I had of Lionel's in 1903; and I am afraid I never expect to see them again.[1] If you come to Oxford at any time, I will show you a tiny portrait I have: quite

[1] These letters were returned by Mr. Frederic Manning, Mr. Galton's executor, in 1923.

unsatisfactory, but the only thing to be had, and impossible to be reproduced. I am just giving up my house here . . . and intend to be "of no fixed abode" for about a year. It is just as well to be unsettled while all England is so: may St. George protect her!

Before I end I must tell you of two especially good provincial booksellers: *i. e.,* Hitchman, Queen's Row, Bristol; Grant, King George IV Bridge, Edinburgh.

Yours sincerely,
L. I. GUINEY.

To A. K. Gibson

HENDERSICK, LOOE, CORNWALL, *July 1,* 1915.

DEAR MR. GIBSON,—If you were over here, and it were after this colossal war (St. George for England, to smash the Hun's ideals!) I do think you might get some of Lionel's *Catholica* printed in a small edition. They are get-at-able, and, as you say, precious. Yes, Mr. Galton is that hapless Galton who was once not only a Catholic but a priest. He was at New College with Lionel: they matriculated, I think, on the same day, although A. G. must have been at least ten years older. When Lionel died, he was the very first to ask to do the Memoir; and the family, quite, quite unliterary, although of high station, told him he might go ahead. But he didn't, and I am sure never will.

No, dear Sarah Jewett, whom I knew well, was never anything but a pro-Catholic. She had a natural love for the Faith, and was particularly attracted, as some of her stories show, to the character of the Catholic Irish, the

MISS GUINEY

FROM A PHOTOGRAPH TAKEN IN BOSTON, 1899
AGED THIRTY-EIGHT

simple devout peasant stock. She spent almost a year once among them at Bantry Bay. Of Mr. Rolfe, alias Corvo, I never even heard! But you know I am, and have been all my life, a very hesternal sort of person, and my ignorance of the present world of letters "sticks fiery off indeed." I am sorry you were able to buy anywhere a copy of that useless youngster book of mine. It has been wholly out of print since about 1890. The only books of mine I would have discoverable at all are *Happy Ending* (collected verses), *Patrins*, and the three little monographs on Henri de la Rochejaquelein (out of print also), Robert Emmet, and Blessed Edmund Campion. *Goosequill Papers* would be capital to light fires with next winter?

I have written at length, being partly invalided and indoored, but on the mend.

Yours sincerely,
L. I. GUINEY.

To Mrs. P. B. Whelpley

HENDERSICK, LOOE, CORNWALL, *24 July*, 1915.

DEAREST JAY,—It is a Long Time. And I've been thinking of you and wondering how and where you are. Since I've got to feel absolutely myself again, I've been working like the Nick, and really taking practically no exercise, which is wicked, I know: but Oh, the lost weeks that have to be made up, and the furious expenses to be met. Hendersick is a perfect success, so far as I am concerned: cool jolly house, clean as a Convent, a nice May and Clarence, and the finest of fields and cliffs, also vats of junket to wallow in, splendid sleeps, and all the liberty and privacy even I could pine for. For all which I am mighty grateful to you. May herself does my mendin' and washin', capable little critter! and I like the whole tribe. They've got one awful shortcoming in common; and that is, absolute disregard of animals except as property. Not even Ivy's hand has ever yet rested (no, not once!) on any dog's or cat's head. The latter are kept to fight rats, and never allowed indoors. (All day long, I hear "G'won" and "Get Out": the sole speech ever addressed to dog or cat in this house.) They run away like mad when I try to make friends with them. The dog here is "Rover," eight months old, surreptitiously my dearest friend, a terribly affectionate little fellow, and hungry, hungry! and always constipated from never getting anything but skim milk and white bread-crusts. Not even so much as a dish of water is ever laid down for him, but if he happens to be about (and he generally takes mighty good care that he is) when the separator is at work, and the milk is being divided out for us, the young calves, and the special pigs, he is allowed to drink out of the latter pail daily: and of course he gorges, as it is his only meal. They complain bitterly that "Rover" is no good at sheep and cow work, unlike "Ben" and "Shep," quite forgetting that he is 1, only a baby; 2, never taught; 3, in misery all the time with canker in his ear, which of course makes him dazed and stupid. I asked about it. They didn't know, hadn't noticed, etc. (though he shakes his pretty white head nearly off three thousand times a day). I told you about the mother-cat. Both kittens have since disappeared. What about that? "Rats, perhaps; or perhaps she ate them." Poor "Ben" is absolutely bare over most of his black back. The cause? "Can't think." A calf is found dead in the fields, of murrain. "Poor beauty!" says I. "Yes, we're five or six pounds out by that!" answers gentle May. "How are the turkeylings?" says I. "One of 'em's going to die." "Horrors! Why?" "Broke its leg or something." "How long ago?" "Oh, long ago, days and days." "Isn't it eating?" "No, it's going to die." "Could I see it?" I did. Luckily, I had arnica here, and plenty of bandages. Then I got May to help me poultice the poor leg, badly swollen from a cruel bruise, and poultice again, until the discharge came. That young Turk is going to be quite well, and not even lame, tomorrow! and he is a major for courage and sense, and is eating enough now for ten. I'm not so hopeful about little "Rover." Canker takes time to cure, and nobody will ever look at him after I am gone. If I had a house, I'd beg for him. May says she "just hates" him! Meanwhile the poor sweet bewildered big baby spends his nights and days on the wet muddy mat in the porch, never taken for a walk (except by me, and then, do what I will, I can't get him to move from my heels), never spoken to, never pitied. But if he thrusts his nose an inch over the threshold he gets "G'won!" very loud and peremptory. I wish I could deliver him. They'll shoot him else, as useless as a sheep-dog. The one you remember, the first "Shep," was shot because he began to get old! An inspector at Burford once told me that Devon and Cornwall were hells for animals! It was incredible then, but I see what he meant, now that I can gauge the attitude of the Tucketts, who surely must be infinitely kinder than the average. The beasts hereabouts are all so handsome, but the stick is their constant portion. Sarah, the jolly little milkmaid, goes forth to feed her seven calves, and vigorously beats six away from the pail while she feasts one by one in turn, whacks 'em right and left over their darlin' faces and poor little budding horns and soft beautiful eyes. Such are the manners and customs hereabouts.

It rains, rains, rains. But I have seen Polperro, yes! and the first sight from the elbow of the cliff-path, and the tide *was* out, and there were flying clouds, and—gulls! Never saw such intrusive, loud-mannered rascals. A wonderful little place. I have also seen St. Neot's and the famous windows, much more personal and "documentary," than Fairford, but not half so fine in design and colour. Lastly, May drove me last week to Fowey, where she had business. I left my heart *there,* sure, with a little harbour with deep waters, and rocky, woody shores, and funny little stubby castles on either entrance-headland, where they used in old days to swing a chain across at night, just as at Dartmouth. It really *is* Dartmouth on a tiny scale. Fowey for ever! Heaps of love to you and P., Miss Wyeth, and the Min. And here endeth Vol. XXVI.

L. I. G.

To The Rev. G. Bliss, S. J.

HENDERSICK, LOOE, CORNWALL, 1915.

. . . My old friend Lionel Johnson once wrote to me: "when I'm dead, the colon won't have a friend in the world but you." He didn't know it was to have a Jesuit friend to whom I might make that same wail and congratulation! You wouldn't believe the things printers are given to cope with. I assure you our MSS. will be Paradise to them, just as they are. Typing would be a big, and absolutely wasteful expense. I suppose your idea is to have the raw material of our book a perfect work of art in itself. Adorable ideal: but "it isn't done!" Do tolerate some messiness, seeing it must evaporate as soon as touched . . . if messes do that!

I'm in rude health again, and I do wish you in a like fix!

Yesterday I got into Pelynt Church, and nearly never emerged, the epitaphs, running from 1610 to 1660, were so fascinating. Nameless magic in them all, as befits the time. On a Trelawney tomb, 1632, some moral reflections, ending:

"Mud-wallèd men, e'er we can mount on high,
Wee cope with Change; wee wander, alter, dye."

And this delightful thing, 1654:

"Thy rest gives mee a restlesse life
Because thou wert a matchlesse wife!
But yet I hope againe, to see
That Day of Christ: and then see thee."

And a half-dozen more. Darlin' old ancestors! They make one forget submarines and flies and no £: s: d:, and one's owne sinnes,—almost. *Saluti.*

L. I. G.

Just a line, because I lo'e ye sae weel for cycling past

Burns' silly old cottage! Can't stand Rabbie nohow,—me that had one Hieland grandmither. . . .

To Strickland Gibson

80 KINGSTON ROAD, OXFORD, *Aug. 8,* 1915.

DEAR MR. GIBSON,—I am back in temporary digs after months of absence, and hear that Mr. Madan is away. I wanted to ask him, or "sound" him, rather, about the admission to work in Bodley of two most uncommonly nice boys. May I see you instead? (*wot larx for me!*). . . . I can forecast some difficulties, yet I hope I may with a moderate degree of confidence bespeak your interest in Edward (15 yesterday) and Gregory (12) Macdonald. To my possibly partial mind, these are born for Bodley. . . .

Every best wish there is from

Yours ever sincerely,

L. I. GUINEY.

To Strickland Gibson

80 KINGSTON ROAD, OXFORD, *Aug. 12,* 1915.

DEAR MR. GIBSON,—That advice is of the best. I will get Edward to write to Mr. Madan, and to be foxy enough to give the latter a few days' rest after returning to a desk doubtless piled high, and not calculated to put one in a really after-dinner mood. Edward hasn't, I fear, any "strong point" or hobby, but he has very perceptible conscience and intelligence, and would do well whatever he is told to do, I know. He is big and grave for a boy just fifteen.

I have a friend in U. S. A. [F. H. Day] who is also

a distant relative: rather a "crank," but made up of goodness, who has collected Keats material from boyhood. I suppose he has the best private Keats collection extant. He talks of adding it to the MSS. which Sir Charles Dilke gave the Hampstead Library (he knew Sir Charles) and I have been writing the hottest kind of a plea, since he asked my opinion on the subject, that the gift shall be diverted to Bodley. *Vedremo!* Put the "pious intention" into your prayers.

Yours ever,
L. I. GUINEY.

To The Rev. John Edge, S. J.

HORTON, PORTEYNON, GOWER, SO. WALES, *Oct. 4*, 1915.

DEAR FR. EDGE,— . . . The Bollandists (if one may be so disrespectful) are next to no good in regard to several Saxon saints, S. Frideswide among them. *E.g.*, apart from making no original investigation whatever on the vexed 'Algar' and 'Bentona' questions, they have copied wrong about every single proper name in Prior Philip's *Book of Miracles*, still preserved in Oxford. To answer the objections as I can: 1. It was with deliberate intention that I slurred the question of the date: and this because I am certain (in my own mind) that the usual 735 and 750 A. D. are wrong, and that our Patroness lived at least a century later. But as I haven't yet got documentary proof, probably never shall get it, and can only offer, when I edit my papers, some strong cumulative probabilities and guesses, I don't parade my theory of the date. The dates 735 and 750 do belong to Queen Frithogith of Wessex, and are appended to charters signed by her. One of the signatures known to be hers is actually written as "Frithuswitha" Regina! I believe this the origin of the mix-up. I wonder if the Benedictines would incorporate and use a vague date, such as "in the latter days of the Heptarchy"?

2. Order of events. I'm awfully sorry; it seems so impudent, indeed, to disagree with the Bollandists. But I suppose I may truly say that I have examined more old MSS. than ever fell in their way (twenty-two or three Lives, besides heaps of scattered notes) and these disagree mightily about the order of events in regard to the taking of the veil and the pursuing prince. I have tried to strike an average and make a statement accordingly.

3. Binsey is a "sell." I am sure S. Frideswide never lived there in person as a nun: it was no safe place, for one thing. Doubtless the Austin Canons who succeeded her community at Christ Church built the Oratory, and carried her cultus thither. Binsey has been indeed confused with "Bentona"; so have Bampton and Bensington. I know where the real Oxfordshire "Bentona" is, and the real "well" is thereby, and *bears today* S. Frideswide's name in a corrupted form. This place answers in every way to the old description of "Bentona." Just fancy anyone in need of water in water-logged Binsey!

4. The "records" (that is, some 14th and 15th century ones) do put *the* well, the miraculous one, I mean, at Binsey, just as some put it at Bampton; and in each place there *is* still an ancient well round which religious traditions centre. But these wells have NEVER borne S. Frideswide's name, and have no more to do with the "Bentona" well than they have with the Tre Fontana.

Perhaps Dom Dominic Wilson might possibly like to see my three long *Tablet* articles on S. Frideswide. Have you got them? and if so, could you furnish the dates? I can't. About 1912? I say this because I should really like him to see that I don't want to be rashly speculative or *entêtée*. He is going, I hear, to use, at least as an alternative form, the proper and original "Frithuswith." . . .

Yours always,
L. I. GUINEY.

To The Rev. John Edge, S. J.

Oct. 8, 1915.

Thank you, dear Fr. Edge, for your letter. . . . I rather wonder at myself for never having told *you*, a real Oxford antiquary, about the place of the [St. Frideswide] relics: it is a bit of most authentic information which some day I will print. Do you remember Mr. Herbert Hurst (B. N. C.) author of *Oxford Topography?* Well, his daughter Gladys . . . told me this. In 1880 Mr. Park Harrison was discovering, and putting together, those blocks of the old Shrine. He had asked Christ Church to help him, as the whole thing was a big expense, but Ch. Ch. never gave one farthing, so he had to go on all on his own, with his friend Mr. Hurst to egg him on, and with nobody at Ch. Ch. caring a straw except Canon Bright; very keen *he* was over the whole business. Mr. P. H. had a strong theory that the old Shrine stood just where it is now, and he believed that the relics lay there under the flooring. You know what a masterly guesser he was. So he got permission to dig. It was done in winter, after dark. The Canon was there, also Mr. Hurst; and the latter brought Gladys, then a child. They found the bones not far below the surface! wrapped in a leather bag, folded. It seems queer to add that those three learned persons knew so little of local Reformation history that, seeing two distinct sets of bones, a large set and a small, they concluded them to be S. Frideswide's and her father's![1] They put them back under the pavement, absolutely certain now where to erect the fragments of the Shrine. Canon Bright, a very enthusiastic man by nature, wrote the inscription, and had the brass tablet repaired, intending to have it clamped down on the flat slab which forms the top of the sub-structure; but he found that Messrs. Harrison and Hurst would not hear of it, on the ground that tourists, &c., would be covering the precious Shrine-base with their initials, once it was labelled. So they made him stick it on the pavement, under the central boss of what was once the Lady Chapel! I used to break my head over the "*subtus*," not knowing how on earth Canon B. could be so sure of the exact locality, and I spent a lot of valuable time hunting up his relatives, &c., and asking in vain for light. It was all plain enough when, by great luck, I mentioned the subject, soon after her father's death, to Gladys Hurst. You will like to know all this. Don't bother to make any answer. As ever,

L. I. G.

---

[1] The bones of a notorious ex-nun were mixed with those of St. Frideswide by the Reformers to prevent veneration.

To Clement Shorter

HORTON, PORTEYNON, GOWER, SO. WALES, *Oct. 20,* 1915.

DEAR MR. SHORTER,—I don't mind in the least being "turned down," but I did think, owing to all the talk about the Mons "angels" &c., that that old Edgehill ghost-story had considerable pertinence. It would quite hurt me if you believed, as you almost seem to imply, that I could be unfeeling in regard to this war. Why, it has had me by the very heart-strings since Aug. 4, 1914! Besides my life-long love of England, I have ever had one overmastering dislike of every Teutonic ideal, the political one not least: I never met anyone in my life who so hated Germanism, root and branch, save Lionel Johnson.

As you're putting me on the defensive, I shall have to protest that I love ye true. I have not set foot in London since the night I called on Dora. My hostess, that brilliant Mrs. Thayer (a great admirer of D's verse), is anything but a "new friend," in fact, we were girls together, when D. was in the cradle, or not very long out of it! My love to her. I gave up my Oxford house nearly a half-year ago, and have been away, mostly in Cornwall and Wales, since then. This wild, lovely, but beautiful coast is the best thing ever for my young cousin, who is not very strong. We go back to O., to lodgings somewhere, in another fortnight. No: pray don't imagine for a moment that I can change towards old kind friends: it isn't in me. But I can't visit or be social as I should like well enough to do, were "cirks" other than they are. You see I have played up frankly to your frank letter. *Addio, Felicità!* Yours as ever,

LOUISE I. GUINEY.

To The Rev. G. Bliss, S. J.

HORTON, PORTEYNON, GOWER, S. WALES,
All Saints (*dear Feast!*), 1915.

DEAR FR. BLISS,—You should get the Prefaces back from Longmans this week. I asked 'em to return same to your address. Let me know if they fail, and I will bomb Pasternoster Row. Tell me, too, if they found Fr. Devas's verses: I am almost as anxious as you must be. (The *Tablet* one is full enough of heart to make one sniffly.) I did, and do, apply for St. Anthony's good offices.

About the mushrooms, we've gobbled another lot of *coprinus comatus* since I wrote! Nothing jollier, stewed in much milk with a little butter and salt. The old ones have black fringes, and are no good to pluck; and all of 'em have to be scraped before cooking. They grow sometimes on lawns, but generally in waste places among bracken, in moist soil; their time is late August–October. Besides the real shaggy-manes, always fuzzy, . . . there is *congregatus*, and *atramentarius:* both of the same general shape and crowded attitude, but brown, not white, and smoother and smaller, and dripping off, when past their prime, into the same dark mess. These are edible too, but not nearly so delicious. I used to know more about these things than I do now, but I am still sure of about twenty kinds to eat, of which I really like about nine. They say there are 252 (!) edible kinds in England. The next time you pass any white puff-balls (if not white they're going to seed) do gather 'em; there are NO poison puff-balls. They have next to no flavour, but they're jolly good at absorbing one: *e. g.*, when roasted, having been skinned, in a dish with a joint. Endeth the mycologic soloist. . . .

To Edward Guiney

LONGWALL COTTAGE, OXFORD, *Feb. 24*, 1916.

. . . So you are back in your pro-German native town? [Cincinnati]. Well, never mind. Nobody is ever sorry to be at the post of duty in obedience to the plain Will of God. But don't lose your dreams, even if they refuse now to take tangible shape. Hold on to them hard. Just so long as we have hunger and aspiration in us, we are *alive* through and through. A college education may not, after all, be the real means to your end: although I am a great believer in University training, particularly as understood over here, where there is so much less distraction and restlessness in things of the mind, and so much graver stress laid on mental character. If you love study, and think and read all you can, you will achieve a real culture of your own, all grain and no chaff. I am so glad you prefer the classic and historic writers in English, and are not dried up intellectually with that deplorable cult of the contemporary which makes so many would-be readers all shallowness and unwisdom. I have always found, and still find, just as much delight in history and antiquities as in poetry. If you were here, I could show you exquisite ancient things on every side. Have you written nothing of late? You may count on my interest if ever you feel inclined to show me anything of that sort. In that case, you must tell me whether you like candid criticism, for your Cousin Lou is "indifferent honest" indeed, as Hamlet says, in that regard, and has the reputation of being a hard hitter, and also (I hope), of loving dearly, when it is to be had, "the noble pleasure of praising." I think you express yourself very lucidly. Your handwriting is lucid too (except for the horrid Greek e's) and it would get to be a distinguished hand if only you would make it a bit smaller, and make it taut, as seamen say, by lessening all the spaces, both of letters in a word, and of words in a line. Hardly anyone in this generation writes an individual hand. In old times all this was an art.

It is pleasant to hear that your little brother is likely to become a really good musician. But before he begins to "make a name," don't you think, doesn't your mother think, that he ought to drop that "Xavier"? I hope I am not lacking in admiration and veneration for the wonderful soul and career of the great S. Francis Xavier, but his second name (or any like it, such as Loyola, de Sales, Neri, &c.) is a terrific handicap in the secular walks of life. And I thought your dear father had named him Francis *Robert?* a name dear to me, and one of our own family names. My cousin Leonard bears it, but is not called by it; but though it was only my father's second name he *was* called by it. His first name was Patrick, and all grandfather's boys (six,—four died young) bore "Patrick" as one of their names . . . and my father never slurred his first name, though some would consider *that* a handicap, but always wrote his name P. R. Guiney. Xavier is different. It is like a foreign label, and queer to spell, or to hear spoken. . . .

We are having our English winter now, this late. The first snow appeared yesterday, and (a most unheard-of thing here!) it has turned out a quite deep snow. And Oh! the heatless houses are cold. An open grate does so little but blink pleasantly, and delude you by looking warm! I am not nearly as well as I usually am, either. I am sorry you are not of a robust constitution: I fear we are all in one boat, in that regard. Do you get enough (1) exercise? (2) sleep? With these, one can at least secure evenness of health and spirits, which is next best to great vigor. I am an enthusiastic out-of-doorer when I get time, and love long walks. But I am also a very busy person, and have hard work to break away often from a heaped-up desk.

You see your letter wasn't half so full of I's as this one is! If we only were acquainted face to face, the I's would soon dwindle. . . .

Yours affectionately,
L. I. GUINEY.
alias COUSIN LOU!

To A. K. Gibson

175 WOODSTOCK ROAD, OXFORD, *May 29,* 1916.

DEAR MR. GIBSON,—You will pardon, will you not, the very worst correspondent going? I did get both your former letter, and that of April 7th, and both were a pleasure to me; but I am such a hard-working being, at desk-tasks of one kind or another almost every minute of every day, year in, year out, that I never can be half so civil as I should like to be to my friends who write to me: I hate a pen as I do a Hun, for the most part. A namesake of yours, Strickland Gibson, an old Oxford friend of mine, and one of the gentlest scholars of the staff of the gentle and scholarly Bodleian Library, went off yesterday to "The Warres": and blue enough these goodbyes make one feel. I am so glad you pray for victory, and no compromise about peace!

Your surmise about poor Dr. Hitchcock is quite correct. He ran off into blatant Modernism, and was inhibited some two or three years ago. You are such a reader of English Catholic journals, you probably know the *New Witness,* Cecil Chesterton's, and an excellent work it is doing, *not,* of course, as an exclusively Papistical sheet. Tell me sometime whether you ever go to Cincinnati? I have a cousin there, a bookish one, who may be about your age, Edward Guiney: I should like him to meet you.

Longmans has brought out a sweet book at a low price, called *A Mediæval Anthology,* edited nicely, but not perfectly, by Mary G. Segar, a Catholic and a charming girl. I think you would appreciate it.

Verdun holds wonderfully, and all's well on the sea. The sadness all about is a confident sadness. Every kind of best wish to you from

L. I. Guiney.

To Falconer Madan[1]

GRANGELEIGH, AMBERLEY, GLOS., *Sept. 14*, 1916.

DEAR MR. MADAN,—I am posting a parcel to you for Bodley, if indeed it be acceptable. There isn't in it one thing of real value, but there are several privately-printed verses which I am fairly sure won't, at any rate, be duplicates of what you have. . . . Inside the packet is an envelope containing two old photographs of Adelaide Neilson; the Hope Collection may like to have these. Then there is, under separate cover, a roll with two more prints for the Hope Collection; this I have also ventured to address to you, as it contains a photograph which you may be good enough to admit into your own Oxford collections: if you want to do so, it would please me well.

Whatever you find no use for, you can fire back at me when I come up for a read sometime in October. . . .

Ever sincerely yours,
L. I. GUINEY.

To Grace Guiney

[*Early in* 1917.]

Gigia mia, not waiting to hear from you, I thought I'd tell you what Dr. Michell Clarke says, as Dr. Bletchley read his letter (or most of it) to me this morning. Now said Dr. M. C. is really the great Dr. we thought him, and chiefly because he takes back "on mature reflection" one thing which he said to us. I do love people capable of doing that, especially people

[1] Bodley's Librarian in succession to Mr. Nicholson.

who really know. He says I have suspicious eyes and ears, and must when able to see both Mr. Adams [the Oxford oculist] and Dr. Pritchard [the London aurist], *but:* he now diagnoses the true cause of the row as vascular lesion at the base of the brain, which strikes me as infinitely more of a bull's-eye hit. He says this on reconsidering (a) that I never had this kind of thing before, though familiar enough with middle-ear divilmints; (b) that the localised discomfort, not pain, relieved in some degree by thermogene for a fortnight & more before he saw me, was high at the nape of the neck and nowhere else; (c) that I felt at no time, as in aural vertigo, a rotary motion. So now he prescribes some awful stuff or other (it has nux vomica, bromide stronchium, and some phosphates or phosphites) 3 times a day for a month, and some other stuff not so strong for two months after! plus a calomel pill every other night, which ought to delight Aunt Kitty. He repeats the permission to work an hour each A.M. and P.M. (Oh, that I could begin *now!!*) & increase as I find I can, but to keep out-of-doors all I can. I am never to STOOP, in or out! So Annie may drop my flower-seeds in the holes I dig, and Wee One [the cat] may button my gaiters, and pick up my hanky when I drop it. I am to steer clear of all excitement and worry, also of all jollification!! Goodbye to dog-fights! And he repeats his most welcome dictum that sharp as my nerves are, there's no organic disease in 'um. However, a leaky brain isn't much of an exchange. I'm a bit slowed down again today, and couldn't finish reading the paper. Annie says she'd love to take care of Baby [Loulie] plus house if we get a house. . . . We shall see.

To Grace Guiney

GRANGELEIGH [AMBERLEY GLOS],
Sat. eve. [*Spring of* 1917.]

. . . Dr. M[ichell] C[larke] was nicer than ever, did all the examining tricks over again, &c., finding much improvement, and says I should be O.K. in another weary month. However, I may stop the d—— medicine next week, and go in for a tonic he gave me, to be kept up until I feel like a "loin chop." Also, he leaves the matter of getting up immediately after, or before, brekker., as also the more important matter of going to Mass, entirely to my discretion after next week. Then he wheeled up his chair, caught me in the eye, and laid down two immutable laws. (1) I'm to clear out by July, and go to the sea!! for two mths "at the very least." All very nice, sez I, just what we pine for; but I must let my 'ouse first. That won't be hard, sez he. Advertise in the Bristol papers, and when you will, give me a description of it, and I'll "boom" it among my patients! So far, so good. I haven't energy eno' to tackle the correspondence yet, but I've found on the map several likely-looking beachy places in Glamorgan, beyond Cardiff, inexpensive to travel to from here, which are within a very few miles of both railway and our Church; and they look wild. F. A. C[rocker] would love the sea; good for you, too, and good for Loulie and Bitsy [the cat]. I'll follow this up later. (2) When I do begin to work, I'm to go ('orrors!) b rule; never more than three hours' consecutive writin'. He suggests a schedule of 3 hours in A.M., 2 hours in P.M. (3 to 5), and an optional hour in evening, as a maximum. But I can read (when fully sot up) more or less as I like, and discriminate between light skirmishing such as letters, &c., and a real bombardment of work. He threatened me with "early" extinction unless I stuck to this in future, and eschew all worry and excitement. Says I have nice sound "young" organs, and nervous energy of the best so far as it goes, but that my *quantity* of it is small, and I have long been overdrawing. Says Pritchard agrees it was vasc. lesion, and that it might have been a lot worse. Says one proof his diagnosis (M. C.'s) was right, was that I'm not delivered by now from difficulty in writing, as I should be if the now relieved ear was the sole cause of the row. (In fact, I've done this letter off and on since 1.30 P.M., just about as I had to do a month ago.) Says I may do gardening ad lib., and may stoop "moderately" but not in the hot sun. Says "that young cousin of yours is inclined to be pessimistic" (about me, I suppose, ye limb?) and that I'm to "buck her up." Oh! This last at parting. Amen. Alleluia. Now for life, and the Good, the Beautiful, the True, with patched-up brains.

I've asked Aunt K. [Mrs. Macdonald] here again, for her own sake, and hope she'll come. . . .

If *you* can find a tenant for July-Aug., or even July-Sept., remember you're in for £1 bonus. . . . Lusty [the old gardener who came twice a week] is here, and there's a sweet quiet little rain on, but I'm very warm and clad in sandals. Annie and Wee make scenes [of affection] daily, almost hourly. The former has no opinion o' me because I waived my dinner today and yesterday. Heat, I suppose, or the bore of having meals when you're not hungry. Do you get enough at Sidesia? [Her name for the Oxford boarding-house where G. G. was staying.] Mrs. Sides told Mrs. Hurst that they were all "just delighted" to have a Gumpy again. Love to 'um, also to George [de Serionne]. Has he told you why he was rejected [for the Army]? It is disquieting. I do hope poor Dick [Bolton, then imprisoned in Germany] won't lose his parcels, espec. the khaki shirt one. But will those Huns forward? Thine,

C. L.

To The Rev. A. F. Day, S. J.

GRANGELEIGH, AMBERLEY, GLOS., *June 11,* 1917.

DEAREST FATHER,—I was so glad of your letter, and the news. May all go well in the bell tent! and ever better. My old advice to you about the Pauline "suffering fools gladly" doesn't extend to heat and flies. Nothing on earth more intolerable. Please don't blame your too-long previous J. C. F. S. D.[1] for helping to floor me: never was there so welcome and light a job, and my one big regret is that I left the Index so faulty after all.

I wonder if you said Mass for me the 2nd of June? For on that day I got well!! just about as suddenly as I fell ill fourteen weeks before; nor have I had a single set-back since. But of course I haven't dared do any real

[1] *The Life or Sir John C. F. S.* (Mr. Justice) *Day, by one of his sons* [A. F. Day]. Heath, Cranton & Co., 1917. L. I. G. did much of the arrangement, revision, etc., of this book.

work yet. The Dr. says "Sea for at least six weeks." Argal, I meekly proceed to let this wigwam if I can, and betake me to the nearest coast of any character, which is So. Wales. You shall hear, if I do. Grace is here for the week-end. She is cataloguing and secretary-izing for Blackwell in Oxford, and loves it. We had a sweet outdoor Corpus Christi Procession through the immense gardens of the Priory yesterday morning. It was my first Mass (imagine!) since mid-winter, though I have got over three or four times in between, to Benediction or for a Visit. . . . How is dear Mary? Will you send her my love?

Your ever-beholden
L. I. G.

To The Rev. A. F. Day, S. J.

GRANGELEIGH, AMBERLEY, GLOS, *July 5*, 1917.

DEAREST FATHER,—I was so glad to hear again from you. I saw in the *Tablet* the notices of your nephew's and Winnie's brother's death, and I felt at once that your first thoughts would be just what you now say of it: "A fine ending." Indeed it was that: one cannot but be proud that the good name has been laid down on the field of honour. What a sweet surprise for Capt. Day, to welcome his first soldier descendant! But will you tell my unforgotten young friend Winnie that I grieve for her too? I know she will take any loss nobly, and see the earthly and heavenly glory of this one. *Requiescat.*

That Ismailia is more "fresh-airish" than Alexandria for you is great news. What do you hear from Fr.

Henry, a hardened campaigner by now? Will you remember me to him sometime? For myself, I am (probably thanks to your Masses and to little else) immensely better since June 12 or 13. In fact, I can now do anything I like except what I most want to do—work! The Drs. (all three, the specialist, the local one, and my aurist) told me to set a slower pace for myself in future. With the best will in the world, I find, to my consternation yet amusement, that I can't! that I must *run* up stairs, etc., to my dying day. So I am compromising, by maintaining my old speed, yet learning, unwillingly, to set up many halts instead of always going express from London to York, *e.g.*, I am adopting the loathly habit of lying down for an hour after the noon meal, and of stopping doing anything the moment fag sets in. A Russian Revolution is small potatoes to that! July 17 I am off to So. Wales, per order, and the last order, I hope, to revel seven or eight weeks in the brine. . . . Grace is to join me, and our small Loulie-cousin, and I have succeeded in letting this house.

I doubt if you have seen this splendid utterance of General Smuts, so here is a copy. What a vision the man has! This morning's paper reports a fine hot scrap at sea between the U. S. A. flotilla crossing to Brest and the submarines, with not a casualty of any kind on the non-Hun side. *Addio, felicità.* A heartful of thanks for the prayers. Yes, I am in a fair state spiritually; full of *confidence* in Almighty God, at any rate. (I often fail just there.)

Your ever devoted

L. I. G.

To Winefride Day

23 Glanmore Crescent, Uplands, Swansea,

17 August, 1917.

You dear Mary,—I was so glad of a sight of your big hand-writing again! The letter and the enclosure reached me here, and I am ever so much obliged for them. In the same post (an odd coincidence!) came my own letter, which I send on, and which you needn't return, as I have copied the address. The next time you write to our Holy Lander, will you enclose, from me, the little old verses by James Day? I often copy for the *Ave Maria* quaint bits like that, which I run across in my Bodley readings. But it is nearly a year now since I was there. I felt ill early in Feb., and began to "come to" in June, and have been climbing up steadily ever since. I am really entirely well now, only I can't do any head-work even yet. The great Dr. [Sir William] Osler of Oxford recommended me to Dr. Michell Clarke, 28, Portland Rd., Clifton, Bristol, as "a brain and nerve specialist whom nobody in all Great Britain can touch," so I went under his care. I pass the recommendation on to you, if ever you or anyone you are interested in, gives out in that way. Unlike Dr. Pritchard (still merrily going it, by the way) he isn't a pre-historic antiquity, but somewhere about fifty, most kind and gentle, and modest to a degree about his own eminence.

I had no pain from first to last, but all the wind went clean out of my sails for many a weary month. I left home on the 14th because Dr. M. C. ordered me to the sea, for the final lap of convalescence, but I couldn't get either a house or lodgings to suit, everything hereabouts is so egregiously crowded. However, I don't dislike Swansea, and on the 31st I can have a nice little cottage at Horton, on the Gower coast, which I have had before; and there my invaluable general, and Grace Guiney too, will join me for a month, so all is well. What a dear you are to suggest Lyme Regis! I have never forgotten the beauty of it, and of that Sunday with you. But I'm tied now, you see, to Horton. Were I there in L. R., I should enter at once as your pupil, and pitch in vigorously as apprentice carpenter. You can do the very nicest manual jobs of anyone I know: book-binding and carpentry are things I have longed all my life to learn, and somehow or other have never got the leisure or opportunity to master. *Splendid* war-work, yours.

You don't say how Fr. Henry is, but evidently you are under no great present anxiety over either brother, and I am so glad for that.

Will you remember me sometime to Mrs. King? I was driven through Bath in a taxi, on one of my visits to Dr. Michell Clarke, and thought of her, especially as Grace (on whose stalwart shoulder I reposed) had missed an arranged-for call on Mrs. King last winter by her own succumbing to pleurisy. These are times. But we are all going to win through soon. I can't bear the Holy Father's peace talk. The criminal in the case is treated by him exactly on a level with the victimized nations, and no settlement is possible until the former is repentant and well-punished by having his claws cut, surely. Ever with love,

Yours, dear Mary,
L. I. GUINEY.

To The Rev. G. Bliss, S. J.

4 CHURCH WALK, OXFORD,
St. Barbara her Feast, 1917 [*Dec. 4.*]

Oh, padre, it *is* you, isn't it? Uncanny, these long flashes of silence; but they don't matter. You're there, and I'm there. And I'm terribly glad to hear you've done the *Morality* [Play].

Well, I felt corkish in Sept., and started in on *the* job again, just managing to mess the pages up, when— BANG! more sky-rockets in my 'ead. Then no-good-ism, and more Drs. rising up like cursed apparitions, and London this time, and threat of the mastoid operation: whereupon my spunk rose toppling high, and I swore no. I am in Oxford, forbidden Bodley, to be sure, but feeling around for a dash at it in February. I go home on Sat'y, cheerful as larks and mighty as lions: really. And I'm just going to beg you to let me uncoil that MS. once more, before you get it for top-polishings. Will you? I've kept it shrouded in wrappings, but directly under my much-prorogued and long-baffled eye. Never say die, me. . . .

Suffer a bit longer ("gladly," advises St. Paul) your devoted and backsliding and penitent and game

L. I. G.

To Clement Shorter

GRANGELEIGH, AMBERLEY, GLOS, *Jan. 16,* 1918.

Oh, dear Mr. Shorter, what am I to say to you? I cannot bear to think of your loss, but I do think a great deal of what should be a magnificent comfort and stay to you now: the memory of your own most chivalrous devotion to Dora, which was like a blossomy screen between her and the outside world. It was all of that, and more. I used to feel that she was by temperament so sensitive, so lonely, and so wilful (in a childlike way) that nobody but you could ever have kept her even moderately happy. She had a wonderfully keen appreciation of all your devotion, under the arch manner she always had towards you, in which I delighted. I don't at all know how you are going to pick up life again after losing Dora. May God give you help and strength to do it. I am glad to be able to write, though this is a sad enough letter. (My head gave out just a year ago, and I have only just pulled my wits together, and escaped from the doctors.) I hope with all my heart you may keep well, and summon up all your courage, and go forward with your good work for English letters. With truest sympathy,

Yours always,
L. I. GUINEY.

To The Rev. A. F. Day, S. J.

AMBERLEY, GLOUCESTERSHIRE, *Easter Tuesday,*
[*2 April*], 1918.

DEAREST FATHER,—I was glad enough of your line of Feb. 19; it came not so long ago! Meanwhile, you will have had a long script from me. These are such heart-shaking days of war again that one is always thinking of one's dear folk over seas. I got my long-deferred Bodley "read" at last, going up three weeks ago, and staying a fortnight, getting home unimpaired too, except for a dust-beridden throat. Sir Walter Gray and Canon Scott Holland died while I was there. One day I ran up against a smart-looking naval gentleman in St. Giles, who turned out to be—Willy![1] Of course our talk was instantly of you; and I had the satisfaction of giving Willy the news,—it was news to him,—of Fr. Henry's M. C.[2] He whistled, for pride and pleasure; also, he recognized how furiously jealous the M. C.'s little brother must feel!! Thank you for that *Observer* cutting. I once flew at nice Katharine Tynan Hinkson, for calling me "Irish-American." Mr. Roosevelt himself doesn't hate a hyphen more. And my father hated it before me. In any case, as I told K. T. H., if I am to be hyphenated, I am several kinds of a hyphen, with a Scots and a French near paternal ancestor, and all my English blood on Mother's side! but plain "American" is my due, and suits me well enough. One of the oddest of Irish qualities is this almost universal grabbism: they claim anything and everything which they think in the least creditable! My girl Grace has lately had another set-back, and in consequence another examination by the Dr., who seems amazed at not finding any *active* tubercular spot. Her power of resistance and recuperation is extraordinary.

[1] William Ponsford.

[2] Fr. Henry Day, S. J., received the Military Cross for valour at Gallipoli, where he served as Chaplain to the Forces.

I long desperately to have her drop her Oxford work, and come home to stay: the indoor atmosphere of libraries, etc., is about as bad as anything possibly can be for damaged lungs. Just now she is cataloguing at Brasenose. So far, I have urged in vain; but I mean to win out. The difficulty is of course an £: s: d: one only: so you may pray for me to see my way through: will you, please? G. has "grown up" unconscionably late, and all at once, and is at last as satisfactory morally as she is clever and delightful. I am setting up a dog,—my first small one: a mongrel terrier, very tractable, young, with a most soulful little phiz: name, Batty, as he comes from the Battersea Dogs' Home. I got him partly for a watch, as my nice servant is lonely when I am away; partly as an inducement to G. to take long walks without me, when she is here. I have explained to said beastie that there is a war on, and that he can't be coddled with a menu, and he seems to acquiesce in *any* edict coming from me, whom he already considers as a body of incomparable and irresistible excellence! That faculty for worship is the special endowment of dogs, and is entirely unconnected, in nine cases out of ten, with self-interest. My book has taken a new start (*Recusant Poets,* Fr. Geoffrey Bliss's book and mine). Oh, how jolly it is to be well, and with brain-wheels oiled and running! A quiet Easter here, in raw weather, after a most lovely winter. Benediction for the Allies yesterday and to-day, after Mass. Do send me a blessing.

Ever your devoted,
LUDOVICA.

To Bruce Porter

GRANGELEIGH, AMBERLEY, GLOS, *April 14,* 1918.

MY DEAR BRUCE PORTER,—What will you think of me for never having acknowledged your wedding card, and sent you my most affectionate congratulations? I was ill, ever so ill, for a whole year, with all my writing machinery stopped. It is enraging to have your head caught, as it were, on barbed wires in No Man's Land, while the rest of you kicks lustily, but all in vain! I've been quite well for just two months, but my arrears have snowed me under. It has been in my mind ever so long to send my especial salutation to your wife. Two artist friends of mine told me of late in Oxford what a Dear was "Polly James"; so you see I know her present pretty alliteration, and find it endearing. I consider it a curious lack in my New England life that I never met her. You must give me the best characther you can! May you both be happy and busy, and have enough to eat, and save your souls! and count me ever among your vassals. Do you remember the day you came to Auburndale, looking, as my mother described you at a venture, "like R. L. S."? And the other day when we gadded into Oxford courts and cloisters? Two occasions, ages apart: but such a good stout bridge of friendship between, isn't there?

Are you grown-up enough to escape going to the Front? I hope so. I'm all of a soldier fibre, but I have lost there my seven dearest boys. We get on hereabouts not without anxieties similar to those of the late summer of 1914. But "tails are up," as General

Haig said the other day, of his indomitables. It can all end in only one way. And Oh! the scars. . . .

I wish I were good for an epithalamium. The Muse, you must know, has a centuried pine growing by now upon her grave. *Vale, fratercule, vale.*

L. I. GUINEY.

To Clement Shorter

GRANGELEIGH, AMBERLEY, GLOS, *Aug. 3,* 1918.

DEAR CLEMENT SHORTER,—I am so touched by your gift of a copy of the really precious book, and hardly know how to thank you enough. You have made it so intimate, with all the portraits and facsimiles. K. T. H.'s little note is full of charm, but has not body enough. I wish you had felt able to do it. I hope some day you may give us a real memoir of dear Dora; for hand, heart and mind would go together to make something everlasting, such as her genius deserved. I had never seen the Chancellor photograph: I like it extremely, though the hands are badly posed. I don't suppose anyone ever admired Dora's beauty more than I did! It was the thought of her which always made me wish nature and heredity had taught me to like Sinn Fein. I feel our divergence much, and to keep it under, felt almost grateful to the otherwise most unkind destiny which of late years has moored me far from my London friends.

I often think of you. May your work and your interests help keep your courage firm! I know how lonely the summer must seem without Dora. With many warm thanks and affectionate remembrances, I am ever

Your old friend,
LOUISE I. GUINEY.

To Clement Shorter

GRANGELEIGH, AMBERLEY, GLOS, *Aug. 4*, 1918.

MY DEAR MR. SHORTER,—Only this morning, showing Dora's lovely book to my cousin Grace Guiney, I fell across your note, which was in among the back fly-leaves. You must have wondered at my non-mention of your very kind invitation. I should very much enjoy dining some evening with you. You know how very seldom I get to town; but I may be up in October. It is sad to think of your individual house, so full of charms and surprises, gone out of your hands. But I know Dora loved Missenden best. Please don't say she might have been happier had she not married you. We outsiders can judge of that more accurately than you can. I assure you every true friend of Dora's knew and knows that your devotion gave her a bulwark and a fortress she never could have won alone from the impact of life; and, believe it, we venerate you for that long chivalry.

I'm so sorry I mentioned Sinn Fein again. Its poets go to my heart, at any rate, and their self-broken wings.

Ever yours,
L. I. GUINEY.

To Clement Shorter

GRANGELEIGH, AMBERLEY, GLOS., *Nov. 2,* 1918.

DEAR MR. SHORTER,—If your Christmas and New Year numbers are not closed, would you consider printing this in them? The writer[1] is a schoolboy of 15, who is, I think, going to be Somebody. He asked me, out of his own head, to "send it to Mr. Shorter." The form and point of this are a bit like Abou ben Adhem; but I don't know that that's in its disfavour. You will think me an extremist! for you'll remember that the last verses I forwarded to you were by an old lady of 83: you printed them, too! You see I have none of my own any more. Best and kindest remembrances from an old friend,

LOUISE I. GUINEY.

To The Rev. G. Bliss, S. J.

[1918.]

. . . You seem to have done and left undone a number of things (*à la* Gerard Hopkins) on the exaggeration of the blind obedience principle. I venerate that, but I don't quite admire it, because it isn't playing the game. Getting a gift like the poetic faculty is such a serious job, to begin with: I don't see how anything on earth can justify the treason of disuse, or make it right to look *outside* it in search of purgation, discipline, humility, detachment, and toil towards perfection. They're all so get-at-able then and there. I know this

[1] William Gregory Macdonald, younger son of the late Dr. W. G. Macdonald of Boston.

isn't the old doctrine. But I'll wager my head it's the true one. Any poet who has a religious vocation is thrice lucky; but it does seem cruel to set him, or for himself to choose, "little occasional pieces," instead of his wings. I wonder on what principle G. M. H. went on soaring after bursting seven years' silence with the "Eurydice." I'm ripping glad he did! . . .

Do rub it into your near-Bolshevists what happy conditions England saw in the days of the great Guilds when Faith was in the saddle. Thorold Rogers, at the very end of one of his big sociological studies, sums it up that the ideal time for workingmen, in respect of good wages, good food, liberty, recreation and industrial prospects was in the latter years of Henry VIII! so that the Blessed Reformation came along and blighted it all just at the moment of at-last-attained perfection, and made a mighty quick and thorough mess of it too. What a post-war world it is! We shall see a terrific two-power clash yet, you and I and our juniors, before Satan goes under. . . .

To Mrs. E. D. Jordan

GRANGELEIGH, AMBERLEY, GLOS, *22 November,* 1918.

MY DEAREST MOTHER Jordan and Mary and Alice, don't think I ever forget you, though I am the verra Deil of a correspondent. My thoughts turn to you very particularly because of the epidemic: how I hope it touched neither you nor any one you care for! We came through all that with pennons flying. The end of the war is glorious, but sobering. There is so much to come. There seems to be a general fear that the adored Big Chief W. W. will bring over some too soft-hearted ideas to the Peace Conference. A generous deal of retributive, as well as reparative justice, would seem very much the thing needed. I have lost all the English boys I cared most for. The American casualties are almost incredible. In my own little circle of schoolmates at home, I hear of four already who have given their sons for the great ideals nearly shattered. I hardly know yet where we are. It will seem strange to be able to take a train at normal prices, and spend a night in a village or town without reporting to the police, and see apples and soap and nails and candles in the shops again, and be able to have your watch mended and leather patches put on your boots! None of these privileges will come very soon. I keep well enough, though I can't work as I did before my breakdown two years ago, nor can I get used or reconciled to being tired out. There are MSS. enough to deal with, only I touch them too seldom, being the same crank I always was when worries are in the wind. One (minor) worry is to find another cottage. This one is sold, and we must move in June. Endless enquiry, so far, brings one answer: that there is absolutely no small house, such as we want, to be had! We rather think of getting near Bath. Grace's work, cataloguing and secretarial, would flourish there, we hope. Oxford is too low ground for her and her always delicate chest. She is a dear thing, and we are the greatest chums. I hope you will like the little photographs: would they were more, and better! My old Mary, I want to hear all about school, and Donald and the other big children. When you get in a rowboat, think of me. And Alice, will you distribute my goodwill all over my old B. P. L. haunts? Sprinkling a special blessing on Miss Tenney, and on Miss Rollins when you can catch her. A most happy Christmas to you all, and the best gifts 1919 can bring to the best family I know.

Ever affectionately yours,

L. I. GUINEY.

To Grace Guiney

AMBERLEY, GLOS, *Early December,* 1918.

DEAREST CHILD,—Please ask Mr. Basil Blackwell if he knows or has a book called *Inland Cruising,* a most excellent comprehensive affair, not dry at all, on canal navigation. If not, say I'm dying to lend him mine. . . . I am afraid I must stick to my withdrawal from Oxford, though not necessarily from Oxfordshire. The place is haunted, to me, who have lost too many friends who used to make it lovely . . . and the climate is good for neither of us, unless we were (what we never never shall be) rich, and free at intervals to move about the country. . . .

It is strange about Nov. 11 [on which date, Armistice Day, G. G. had received news of her brother's sudden death while he was travelling in America]. Your getting the news then quite covers it. I suppose poor John lay unconscious in that hotel, and could ask for no Last Sacraments. It is strange, too, that he should have died in Portland, where his grandparents and two young uncles lie. Had I been Leo, I should have laid him to rest there. . . .

Nov. 11 was a black day in a week of much depression; nor have I been able to shake the depression off; and I vowed, to shame myself, if not to dissipate it, that I would tell you that I am on my final legs and know not whither to turn or what to do. For weeks I have been as one dead, or of lead, though perfectly well, and have experienced nothing like it since a November darkness of 1912. . . . I get up betimes and go to Mass; and I go to post at four. I have done literally nothing else for long. The time between I give to—drink: what is exactly equivalent to it, for I am living on Stevenson's wild tales, and have read every word of *Ballantrae* and *The Wrecker* and *David Balfour,* and re-read every word of *Kidnapped* and *The Ebb Tide.* O my old R. L. S.! how I do thank him.

My head and heart are paralysed. I have written *seventy*-odd letters about a house to go to, in vain; and spent over £5 on advertisements, in vain,—which hurts because it is borrowed money, and because I have but £3.4.0 left and cannot borrow again. And time passes and passes, and my work, or what was and yet could be my work, the one thing for which I have a constant passion, lies untouched, week after week, month after month. Many drastic schemes come into my head. One is to sell or pawn all here in the spring, and go off alone, far away. As a choice of workhouses (I'm not joking) I prefer an American one. As to Agnes Purday's things, they weigh so on me, those here and the warehoused ones, that I must chuck them in the next few months, unless she comes or writes to reclaim them. The people I borrowed of are Mrs. —— and Miss ——. It took a terrible lot of debating, this last: yet I knew she had it, and I knew she would spare it to me, which she did, with every expression of kindness. Of course I was badly in arrears when I borrowed: £10 from each. And now I am torn in two because I am not paying back. What with Annie's careful economies, and no other expense on my part except research, I cannot understand money going as it does. It must be the war conditions, as I have never got stuck so badly as this. *Adhaesit anima mea ad pavimentum.* I am a failure, a wastrel, and not one of all my books worth £1 per annum to me. You must forgive all this outburst. Be jolly sure (1) it goes into no ear but yours; and (2) that *I will never forgive you if in any way whatever you lift a finger to alter things.* Let me dree my weird. I've been heading up against the wind very unnaturally for some six years now. Some sort of break-up is imminent, for I'm not getting any younger. I'm like a galvanized corpse kept alive by [others]; but in myself I have no weapon to fight the world with. And my mind is like the "walking-stick" insect, so infernally sensitive that if touched or breathed upon, it can only hang lifeless, instead of scuttling away. Enough, and more, of this.

I wish you'd go and see Aunt Kitty, nominally because I asked you to inquire about Nan (A. K. writes most anxiously about her), really because she wants to be sweet to you, to show you she feels your loss of John. She said as much. Also that you were "so brave and self-contained" it was hard to put into speech her real sympathy. It is such a relief to me that you are in that kind landlady's hands, and away from those Walton Street chunks of muddy ice. Tell me what pretext you gave on leaving. I fear P.'s religion is only a sentiment, and her rock a mere historical Christ dead and gone, with no living divine work and spirit left here behind Him? . . .

What's left of your loving old
C. L.

To Professor Charles Mills Gayley

GRANGELEIGH, AMBERLEY, GLOS, *Dec. 12,* 1918.

DEAR PROFESSOR GAYLEY,—For a long time now I have been intending to venture sending you a few unimportant notes made on your *Francis Beaumont,* a book I admire out of all reckoning. In fact, as a monograph on an English writer of the first class, I doubt if there be any such book extant; and it has for four years been a matter of enormous pride to me that it is the work of an American scholar. I really can't tell you how I rejoice in the clear vision of it, the sweep, the insight, the accuracy, the critical synthesis, the literary charm: and all "soe new, soe fresh, soe nothing trodd upon." This may sound enthusiastic, but only because it has been bottled up. The Great Victory thaws reticences and delays. As I have more than once read the thing through from Preface to Pedigrees, and am always going back to it for reference, I know you will forgive me if I copy now a few jottings made on a paper grey with age (they mostly refer to mere misprints) and send you a summary of some papers from the Recusants Rolls in the Public Record Office. These prove Sir John Beaumont a "Catholique of the Popes church" up to the hilt, and shows what sufferers his wife and children also were for the same cause. My curiosity will some day carry me to search the Southwark and Kentish Recusant Rolls for his brother Francis: a far more difficult quest, I suspect. On the excellent and unimpeachable principle that a thief is the only expert at catching a thief, I might go on to say that Fr. B. has always sounded utterly Catholic to me who am one! But it is dangerous, they say, to go by hearsays. To you, as to nobody else, we owe a clear knowledge of what is, and what is not, his own work, (I'm hard to convince, however, that any adolescent pen wrote *Salamacis and Hermaphroditus*) and such "delimitation" is far more important than biography. But I love grubbing for facts and am ever at it, along one line or another; so if ever I start this golden quarry of yours, I shall be sure to let you know the result. Meanwhile, please accept my thanks and homage, this late, and believe me, with all kinds of good wishes,

Very sincerely yours,
LOUISE I. GUINEY.

P. S. Pray don't leave it to any one else to edit Francis Beaumont. You owe that to him.

Prof. Gayley to G. Guiney, Dec. 16, 1923. "Miss Guiney's spontaneous and generous appreciation of my

Beaumont is the most sympathetic and understanding tribute I have ever received from poet or critic—and she was both. It encouraged me tremendously. Her list of misprints and suggestions for a new edition, and her summary from the Recusant Rolls (P. R. O.) are of invaluable assistance. . . ."

To The Rev. G. Bliss, S. J.

1919.

. . . Thunderstorms, oh yes! I always approved of 'em. But I never recognized that I had said so, frequently, in verse, till you pointed it out. In "Romans in Dorset," too. I actually saw those cloud-heads, crossing Egdon with Alice Brown in 1895 (she did, too), but "The Squall" I saw, and smelled! alone, on a verandah on the Maine coast, in or about 1898. There wasn't any Everard; all piffle. The Ruin sonnet means Rochester Castle. I was there, I think, only that once, quite 24 or 25 yrs. ago. It was raining guns when I started up the stair in the great wall, and as soon as I reached the top there was a magniffy thunder-clap, and a tree got withered just below. I was ashamed that I wasn't scared. I've cultivated "greed of life" since that hour.

. . . What a blessed remark that you love Shirley because he must have hated schoolmastering! for then *you* hate it, and I'm proud of you. My hugged-most bit of Phariseeism is the sense that I never taught nobody nuffin! . . .

To Edward A. Church[1]

GRANGELEIGH, AMBERLEY, GLOS, *10 January,* 1919.

DEAR MR. CHURCH,—Imagine my forgetting either of you! And what a ducky conspiracy you have entered into with my old chum Alice Brown, to pelt me with sparkling cubes of real sugar as ever was! The parcel reached me this day, and had its touch of comedy; for it was plainly addressed, in your own neat unmistakable hand-writing, to Mrs. Gandy! but the tied on label bore my name, and brought the haul to me. So I wrote at once to Mrs. Gandy, to inquire if her little hamper bore a similar double face, and suggested that in such a case we should proceed to devour each other's loot. Thank you a thousand times. I haven't minded the food restrictions much, and the magnificent-sounding raids still less (I was in two, on two successive London nights, just a year ago), but what still gets me, and fills me with language, is the double fare on all railway journeys, and the wholly infernal necessity of reporting to the police if you sleep five miles away from home! This Aliens Law has kept Grace Guiney, my cousin and housemate, and me cooped up for four years, and is not even yet obsolete. Some of us feel extremely sorry the armistice came just when it did, preventing a certain and smashing military victory, which would have really cleared the air in Hunland, and left no such terrific tangles as now beset the Peace Conference on all sides. Of course I can't help looking at things from

[1] This letter refers to some sugar sent to L. I. G. at a time when that article was scarce, and Miss G.'s package went to my Sister in London, Mrs. Gandy—while L. I. G. received that intended for Mrs. G.—NOTE BY MR. CHURCH.

the soldier point of view. We shall see what all the talkers and theorisers will make of it. The few-worded Foch is reported to have said of the many worded Wilson (why, by all that's civil, is he Kinging it over here?) "*Ça m'agace, ces quatorze points. Le bon Dieu lui-mème n'a que dix!*" And I must add a most precious *mot* heard in St. James's Street on Dec. 26, by a great friend of mine, wife of one of our U. S. N. attachés. She was crushed in the crowd against a huge cullud gemman smoking an aromatic cigar into her hat. The President's carriage passed amid indescribable enthusiasm. Instantly, up the empty mid-street came some religious crank or other with a board held high; and on the board was chalked:

PREPARE TO MEET
THE KING OF GLORY

The cullud gemman shouted at once: "Yo' too late, chile: he's jes' done gone by." All of London which could hear and see burst into a thunder-clap of laughter. My love and a happy New Year to Mrs. Church. I keep pretty well, but my head isn't the racehorse it was before Feb., 1917, when I had an odd, extremely sudden, and slow-mending breakdown. I have felt the *fatigue* of reading, and especially of writing, ever since. (You won't credit me, after this boa-constrictor of a letter!) Believe me ever so sensible of your jolly kindness, and always your affectionate old friend,

L. I. GUINEY.

To The Rev. G. Bliss, S. J.

GRANGELEIGH, AMBERLEY, GLOS, *Feb. 5,* 1919.

MY DEAR FATHER,—As I was saying, you'll rejoice with me that I have a G. Hopkins all my own, sent to me by Mr. Milford himself for review, and I'm going to do it in the *Cath. World,* as I did Dolben; ought to have done it, in fact, weeks ago; but I've been moribund, and began to come to, this week. It's the adorablest book. Of the things new to me I'm enormously taken with Binsey Poplars, In the Valley of the Elwy, Handsome Heart, Felix Randal, Brothers, Alphonsus, the Winefride Well Echoes, and of course the "terrible Sonnets." By the way, the sapient Robert Bridges, Hopkins' editor, must be wrong (I'm dying to hear *you* say he is!) about No. 40 (p. 62) being the one "written in blood"; for it is, with all its pain, a paean of "now done darkness." Surely 41 or 45 fits that description? It is a great psychological slip of R. B.'s; but he is amazingly defective in everything dealing with Catholic soul-experience. I find he errs sometimes in technical ways. In 45 isn't it cruelly stupid to stress

> "What hours, O what black hoürs
> We have spent"?

I'll bet my spectacles the author had in mind the "black" as the reverting thought and the laid-over word for emphasis. And in 34 (I love it hard!) line 8 should read:

> "Crying: What I dó is me," &c.?

These are strange carelessnesses. In 41, line 2, do you agree that a "not" is needed before "wilder"? It seems to me imperative. I find I can't go Tom's Garland or Harry Ploughman at all, nor the whole Part I of the Deutschland. Every painting of water is a miracle, from "the rash smart sloggering brine" to the burn with its "windpuff bonnet of fawn-froth." O my zoul! what poetry it all is! I wonder if the behindhand "co-religionists" will make a row over it now, and get the tardy tolerance of the Laureate? How should *he* know whether G. M. H. were appreciated by them or not? As a matter of fact, from the coming forth of Miles' *Poets of the Century* in 1894 the only enthusiasts about G. M. H. whom I have known (and my "circle" was never a predominantly Catholic one in U. S. A.) were all three Catholics. I love the portraits (only the young one is new to me) and I thank God, truly and repeatedly, for that jaw and chin: they mean ballast in threatened shipwreck and anchor in storms. And now Dolben is a book and Hopkins is a book, I feel lonely; for these were the last of my secret admirations. I ought to love the Public Weal more! . . .

To The Rev. G. Bliss, S. J.

Feb. 17, 1919.

. . . I shall be only too flattered to send "Brother" back some day for Fr. Devas to see, and some other dog-scripts too, if you say so. He's my friend for life already, if he's an *animalier*. I can't go the mediæval philosophy of "life as a mode of matter" in the beasties, and "life as a spiritual substance" in we-uns. Life as a communicated attribute of God seems to my untechnical head a grand unifying sort of thing; I don't want to split it up. Neither you nor any S. J. of your group or generation swallows the stuff the Schoolmen wrote and believed about womenkind; then why hang to their myopism in regard to the inferior creation? Do you know W. Clifford Mellor's little book, *A Brief for Animal Immortality?* I have no copy, and can't get one; it's out of print. But it is a luminous and perfectly Catholic plea by a Catholic lawyer, ever so normal and sound and unpolemical. I forget whether he quotes Cornelius à Lapide on Rom. VIII, 19, &c., but he ought to if he doesn't. By Hercules his foot, I wish I could convert you to some post-scholasticism on that mysterious subject. . . .

To Miss ——

GRANGELEIGH, AMBERLEY, GLOS, *14 March,* 1919.

DEAR MISS . . . That you like R. H. Froude, and even my account of him, is truly pleasant to hear; and I thank you much for your letter and for the verses. These last show, (although, as you say, you have not quite mastered your medium,) that you have got to the heart of him:

> "—an aureole
> Of quick and circling words"

hits the mark; and so does

> "A solitary flash out of the dark."

Hurrell Froude is, was, and will be unique and unforgettable to those who love him at all. I am interested in your reference to Saint John's, where I have a very good friend, Fr. Field, S. S. J. E. (I am Boston-born, and lived for years on Pinckney Street.) But why do you say " 'a strong national feeling' keeps you in the English Church"? National feeling is no sort of criterion of supra-national and super-natural Truth. And so thought R. F. H., if you remember! though he did not live long enough to break through. How I wish you may go farther and fare better! and reach the old Home of all true Christian souls.

May I add a word about my own verse? It is: don't waste time on *A Roadside Harp*. All that is best in it (and all my other best) is in *Happy Ending,* published by Houghton, Mifflin & Co., in 1909.

Every kind acknowledgment and good wish from

L. I. GUINEY.

To George Norton Northrop

GRANGELEIGH, AMBERLEY, GLOS, *June 19,* 1919.

You dear boy, this *is* a miss! Why isn't this next week, when I hope to go up to browse in Bodley? or why aren't you staying on long enough to come to this funny little place perched on a Cotswold peak's flank, where I could make you welcome? You are a "moth-eaten old Major" (bravo! that's the sort of poet I like, the Surrey, Sidney, Lovelace breed!) and therefore I gather you are not "demobbed." Tell me how long you will be in England. Try to get here . . . as soon after July 5 as you can; for I could even put you up, and give you our very own radishes for your brekker, and show you a view you wouldn't soon forget. I leave before Michaelmas for—*Plein Air* or the Work'us.

Ah, yes, the golden lives gone since 1914. Only one of those I loved very much, who used to be in and out of Longwall Cottage, has come back. But one walks on always by their light now. . . .

Yours affectionately,
L. I. GUINEY.

To The Rev. G. Bliss

[1919.]

. . . I didn't put Athassel into *Happy Ending,* I seem to remember, because I thought one "Pray-for-me" poem was enough: that one about the sea and the trees and the animals,—I forget its name. By the way, we can't correspond in folios, yet I don't know how I'm going to wait till I can thresh out that big Animal Question with you. Do you remember we started it in the clearing at the end of the Rodborough beeches, with those two infant imps slinging leaves-cum-mud at us? It's an enormous subject, one that goes deep with me. It covers so much of biology, so much of the code of honour, so many implications of theology! And it is either spurned, or messed up with all sorts of silliness. I do live in hope you'll take back one thing you said, a mere rhetorical not-youism: that "an animal is infinitely more like a machine than like a man." Oh, no! for God made him. He has never troubled to make a machine. And there will be no machine in it with the Four Living Creatures singing a man's song in The Day.

I'm a passionate believer in The Day: and I see it as Cornelius à Lapide says St. Paul saw it (Rom. VIII, 19-20) as vocal with all life ever lived. You will have smelled this out in me Works? . . .

To A. K. Gibson

GRANGELEIGH, AMBERLEY, GLOS, *Sept. 16*, 1919.

DEAR MR. GIBSON,—I seize my one chance of answering your pleasant letter of yesterday's post, "or else for ever after hold my peace," as I am likely to be overwhelmed with work of various kinds very soon. But I shall hold this open until I can insert some word from Mr. Elkin Mathews, to whom I am referring your queries. All I know is that he has tried hard, and tried lately, to get out of the Rev. A. Galton's hands the L. J. letters, &c., entrusted to the latter seventeen years ago; but as that worthy still says he *is* going to write the Memoir, the situation becomes somewhat complicated. I have not seen any announcement of the Winchester letters: one would gather they must have been written for his family, or to his mother only. Meanwhile there is a very intelligent Mr. Robert Shafer, tutor at the Naval Academy in Annapolis, who has ready for the press (under what title I know not) a good many of Lionel's essays in *The Academy*, &c., not included in *Post Liminium*. . . . The circle of Lionel's lovers is certainly growing, as it was bound to do!

As to my *Recusant Poets*, Fr. Geoffrey Bliss's and mine, we got together this summer and finished the two big volumes, all but a few loose threads. . . . It is rather against the poor bantling that its two sponsors are exceptionally busy folk, neither of whom can give it continuous ante-natal attention. You will find the subject matter surprising: nearly all quite new (of the old-new kind) and of high average interest and value. It is a book I should dearly love, I know well, if I should discover it as a reader, and a wonderful bit of Catholic life and history.

With all friendly well-wishings, I am yours ever sincerely,

L. I. GUINEY.

To The Rev. G. Bliss, S. J.[1]

OXFORD, *Nov. 24,* 1919.

. . . We lost our dear little fellow a week ago, and Grace and I buried him ourselves in the garden of the Oxford house where he was born, and next to a dog he used to love very much. I don't think you know how much he has meant to us for eight years, with his extraordinary little mind, and his never-failing affection. His responsiveness was like a good dog's, and so was his dependence on, and delight in, the human eye. His going cost us (and poor Annie too) a lot of grief. . . . We buried some purple pansies with him, and this on a card: "G. C. G. and L. I. G. thank God for you, Wee-One, and for much joy in you now taken away." It was a frosty slippery Sunday morning, and though we had ordered a cab, no cabman would take his horses out, so we walked from the vet's, carrying Wee (his poor little

[1] A favorite cat had died.

WESTCOTE, CHIPPING CAMDEN, GLOUCESTERSHIRE, ENGLAND, WHERE MISS GUINEY DIED, 2 NOVEMBER, 1920

(THE HOUSE IS THE THIRD CHIMNEY FROM THE LEFT)

13 lbs. never so heavy before) the two miles. And neither of us could see our spades nor the ground. . . .

To Annie Overton[1]

OXFORD, *24 Nov.,* 1919.

DEAR ANNIE,—I suppose we are all engaged in the same effort, to try to face the loss of our dear little fellow, whose like we shall never see again. Tomorrow I shall buy a few bulbs to plant over him. Don't ever think it could have been "wrong," as you suggest, to have loved him so much and have been so occupied with him. Love is never "wrong" except when immoderate, and in opposition to God's will; but I am sure we are all very grateful to Him for having made Bitsy and given him to us, and that we give him back again, certainly *willingly,* though with real grief. So there is nothing to regret at all in the past. . . .

Keep well. Yours ever,

L. I. G.

To John B. Wainewright

LLANOVER HOUSE, ABERGAVENNY, S. WALES,
Jan. 15, 1920.

DEAR MR. WAINEWRIGHT,— . . . Lastly, I come to our muttons, your enchanting yellow booklet, a gift I am most grateful for. What a beautiful thing to have done! and great fun to have had a go at these slight immortal things so much handled, and to have come off first best! . . . May I say this, that you are

[1] L. I. G.'s devoted housekeeper.

not the hard hunter of s's that an English poet is bound to be? The Theocritus (p. 14), the Horace (pp. 32-33) have only (to me) one flaw: that the lines are unnecessarily sibilant. (Lucky I am writing prose! or I give the case away by that hiss just committed!) Even the all-famous Simonides (top of p. 29) would benefit by "behest" instead of "behests." "Announce" is the very word, or else I should beg you to let the messenger of the heroic dead "take word" or "declare" or even "make known": anything to get three or four s's out of the opening line. Perhaps I exaggerate: s-battues are hobbies of mine. But so they were Milton's. . . .

Do you not agree with me that Lionel's verse "taxes" the ordinary reader? I didn't mean exactly that it is hard to understand, but that it represents a mood and also an ideal which are entirely uncompromising, and which concede nothing to a reader of another tradition. He demands concentrated attentiveness, and rewards it. Fancy H. G. Wells or Mr. Smillie learning L. J. by heart! I see you have used his favourite seventeenth-century metre on your p. 32. It is highly applicable to Horace.

Goodnight. Thank you once more for all your most ready kindness and encouragement. With all best wishes

Yours sincerely,

L. I. Guiney.

To The Rev. G. Bliss, S. J.

Jan. 31, 1920.

You poor Dear, I knew you had got into a hole, and I should like to cuss the grind, the job you were never born to, however fatally well you do it. I say: *will* you take a bit of advice, and act on it? for if you do I promise you a steady inflowing of energy and go. To wit: Open your window wide (I hope you keep one *always* open at night?) when you're half-dressed, and stand near it for just five minutes every morning for leg and arm exercise, not violent, but ordered and persistent. And the same at night, five minutes, for trunk and chest. A *cold* sponge-down after both stunts. Truly, you don't know the power and joy of this little trick. I haven't a doubt such a good vaulter as you are is an accomplished stander-on-his-head? The latter person can always flush and renovate his brain cheap when he feels stale. *Q. e. d.* Do try to be a Good Boy.

Feel quite piggy, me, to get that wonderful bit, "Roger," copied out in your tired best hand. It is all thrills. It struck home sharply to my own experience, for I remember that identical thing (in kind, of course, not in degree) happening to my best dog Brontë, otherwise "Brother," and to me, in the autumn of 1897. In our case it was only flooded fields (a dam had burst), oncoming night, and a sea-coast full of chasms running up far in-shore. There was no time to skirt the chasms, as we had done coming, so going back, I had to climb down and up: and one of them was a big risk. I can never forget B.'s protests and arguments rising to the darkling heavens. He stood on tops of crags and yelled the whole time I was negotiating *my* passage, but only grunted while his own turn came. For the last climb, I lashed my crook stick to a branch with my scarf, and helped him up with it, for it was too perpendicular for his twelve stone, wonderfully light and canny as he always was on his feet: (of course I should have been powerless on that wall without the same strong crook, and unless I had taken my shoes off) and his behaviour at the end of the job was just "Roger's": sheer mad orgies of joy and congratulation, and infinite punching and hugging of the Beloved Object. He *could* have gone round the far point of all the gullies as well as not, for he knew I wanted him to, and he wouldn't have minded the bog: but nothing would have driven him from my side while I was bound on such incomprehensible antics. I think dogs have the sense of danger and the sense of mastery over it as strongly at least as we have, and they are always co-operative in the face of it, especially when the co-op is their human being. I knew two canine chums in U. S. A., one a retriever, one a terrier. The little one got stuck in a woodchuck's burrow, and Beppo dashed back like mad into the harvest-field, to pull sleeves and bark and look S. O. S.'s. Nobody minded, being too busy, but finally a boy was told off to follow him. Beppo took him post-haste to Pat: but poor little Pat, warm and limp, was just dead. . . .

To Edward Guiney

LLANOVER HOUSE, ABERGAVENNY, S. WALES,
March 19, 1920.

MY VERY DEAR EDWARD,—Your most welcome letter should have been answered last month, but I had been working too hard, and had got into the zone of insomnia unawares; and whenever I do that, I am good for nothing by day for a long while on end. But the gap had one advantage: it gave me time to think a good deal about you! and so I did. First of all, I must tell you that Grace and I have given up our dear little house at Amberley: rather, it was sold, and we couldn't stay on, though the very nice new landlord gave us an extra quarter in which to look about in. It was in vain. Not a rooftree, in these queer times, can be had at my very moderate rental. So we must fain continue homeless for the time being, with all my books and belongings in storage. Meanwhile, Lord Treowen (an old Major-General who is a Catholic) wanted Grace to catalogue his library here in a house not occupied, though in perfect order, with a kind little Welsh housekeeper and a maid to man it. So she came on for a six-months' task, and I came with her, only too glad to have the space, quiet, and lonely leisure for my own work. . . . We are almost on the banks of the Usk, clearest and swiftest of streams, and I love it because beside it lived and died my dear seventeenth-century poet, Henry Vaughan. Altogether we are happy, and never lonely, and it is amusing to play at being châtelaines of an old English estate. . . .

Well, now for the matter of your letter. You have certainly had a hard experience, poor boy: one not unprecedented in the Guiney family, where "business genius" is not conspicuous. Be a Pharisee, and thank the Lord you haven't it, being born for better things. I am proud of your non-revengeful spirit; and I see trouble has not soured you in the least, as well it might have done. But what does give me a lot of concern is your health. "Mr. Wordsworth! this will never do," as the famous reviewer said. I have been a delicate person myself, and have reformed, so I speak with some sympathy. In fact, I am going on to say several things, and quite seriously. I am no great hand at circumlocution. One is, that I am very glad your attention is concentrating on rare books and manuscripts, and there I trust it may be enabled to remain, for there are few occupations so satisfying, especially to a naturally bookish person like yourself. But to me it seems plain that our country must for a very long time as yet, offer but second-rate chances to buyers; to sellers it offers the very best chances in the world. Had you ever thought of anything so apparently wild, but so really sane and practical, as getting a knowledge at first hand of the English market? as watching Quaritch, Maggs, Dobell, &c., at work? Do you know any great firm who would send you over here to prospect? If you don't, would you, could you, or ought you to dare take the risk of acquainting yourself, on your own account, with the English book-world? Have you $500 or $600 to play with? By that I mean ready money to invest in a professional scouting expedition, with a fair chance of full returns later on? If you haven't, I don't want to urge your borrowing it (for I hate the idea of borrowing) and yet it is my strong conviction, now at the turning-point of your career, that you could not do a more rational thing than to spend a couple of months here, say next Oct. and Nov., getting into touch with the heads of the book trade, or with publishers of the right kind. I could give you letters of introduction (and almost everything here still goes by private recommendation, not by advertising). . . . I believe it hardly possible that some lasting good should not come of it. Will you think it over? . . . You would make friends, and see and touch the Past, as you never can in our new land. Wherever I am would be your home and headquarters, and my experience, such as it is, would be at your service. So would Grace's, which is of value by now, and lies much nearer your own field of work. Best of all, the change and rest, the quieter and more tranquillising conditions of life here (rapidly breaking up, alas, since the war) would be a great physical benefit. Were I only able to make this possible for you, like a fairy godmother, you wouldn't be long in setting out. But we can only just scrabble along, and have many anxious times. I found I could never make ends meet at home in Boston. Besides, we are both strong and well here, though not there. My girl has long since adopted me as an "Aunt," and so may you, if you ever lay the claim in person, on this side the sea. Is that an inducement? I have a mock-nephew Edward [Macdonald], a boy of nineteen; I should have to call you something else. To wind up with, I should love to see you: for you sound very much mine. Do give some hard thought to the revolutionary programme outlined above. When next you write, put in all the family details so far left out. What is your Louise Imogen up to? . . . and Marie Louise, who told me once, in a letter of her graduation year, that her immediate vocation was to give her brain a rest. I think the hibernation must be over?

This is a very long letter, for me. I shall hope to hear from you soon again. Excellent business,—this helping to found a Poetry Society. Goodnight.

Affectionately yours,
LOUISE I. GUINEY.

To Mrs. P. B. Whelpley

LLANOVER HOUSE, ABERGAVENNY, S. WALES,
21 March, 1920.

Dearest Jay-Thing, you're still a Love to us, and not a Remorse; but a Puzzle too. Do you know I have written twice since Dec. 1? and I think Gi is your creditor too. What are we to hope or fear or believe? I know we want you back mightily; and wait word with ever-diminishing confidence that you're really coming. Do please utter sounds and bridge distances. I expect you *are* doing the latter every day, in these ugly times of anglo-phobiac epidemic amongst our own folk. My young friend Bob Wilberforce has been put in charge of a bureau of statistics, etc., in New York, by the Foreign Office, and is dispensing golden syrup and the milk of H—n K—s to all who come. Poor old England is "muddlin" along, and is much astonished to be thought *persona non grata.* She is, however, drowned this moment in primroses and wild daffies: we've seen 'em, smelled 'em, gathered 'em! Never was such a spring for flowers and lambs and warm blue skies. Where do you think we are until July but at the above pastoral address? Gigi is doing a huge library, one of Lord Treowen's, here in a perfectly kept place empty except for us, and various nice simple kind old retainers, female and male: no servile airs in any, or about as much, say, as these is "side" in us! I was invited to join Gi, and did it unanimously and loudly! I have my own study, and deal with the housekeeper, a ducky Welshwoman, as my landlady. And we are *that* happy, and never lonely, and have a collie to walk with, and a boat on the pond and a fire in our bedrooms: and we NEVER want to "go to England," as they always say here. But there's July, and the end of the job; and a large haze beyond it. Annie continues lent, but is very keen to egg me on into a furnished abode somewhere, since an unfurnished one is about as get-at-able as the moon.

At this moment Gi is in Oxford, on a two days' leave, and I am in Hereford, where I got off her train to look at a seventeenth-century MS. We join up, and return to Abergavenny, with its dear hills and streams (old ground to me) tomorrow. Llanover is four miles south, and there's a pony trap, mind you, with a strong-minded business person in the shafts who was once a wild colt on the Skyrrid Mountain, and there's a sweet old wog on the wiser side of seventy to drive the same: and his name is Reuben Lewis, and the beastie's is Kelly. You'd love the place. The house isn't much, though big: it's "Tudor" of the 'fifties, and has a lot of windows and rows of dull portraits, and wall-papers which are a scream, and some unstrung tall Welsh harps looking very melancholy in a gallery over the hall. But it has a quiet homely unfussed air. The park is full of unexpected streams and rare bushes and trees now all in bloom. There is a circle of nine immemorial wells around a Mound where a hermit lived long ago: hence Llanover, Church of Gover, with the "g" lost out of it. Everybody is old, busy, happy: nobody is ever turned off, and artists aged ninety are still cutting borders and persecuting weeds. There are miles and miles of wire, no inch of barbed wire. The village has an Eisteddfod every year, with prizes, and public criticism of literary and musical efforts. We went to the 1920 one, and fell in love with a determined-looking charwoman who recited The Song of a Million Men with a fiery Welsh accent and vast military spirit. Lord T. is going to have the house repaired as soon as we go: it doesn't need much besides electric light and "decorations." He has other 'omes; got this lately from a grandma. He is a soldier-man, a Catholic, plain as plain, rather taciturn, long known as Maj. Gen. Sir Ivor Herbert; we love the wife; the only son they lost in the war, and it has shaped them both towards an old age perfectly uncomplaining. "No hope can have no fear." The books are many and interesting, and Gi is getting to be a learned bibliographer.

Now my news is done; may we not have yours? I'm ever so well, and the last trailing vertebræ of me are well out of a horrid tunnel of sleeplessness. I'm no thinner, or richer, or lazier. Can't we do anything for you over here? I'm so glad the Min is in clover: but she would barter whole fields of it for a peep at you. Love to Philip (isn't he demobbed yet?) and my blessing to your cherished old self. Yesterday as ever was,

Ralph Cram sailed to join Bess and his girls in Paris, and I shall see him soon; pleasant thought!

Ever your 'fectionate

L. I. G.

To Gwenllian E. F. Morgan

LLANOVER, *April 29,* 1920.

. . . I must tell you that I actually got as far as Llansantffread on Monday last, a very showery chilly day. . . . And I walked straight to the grave and back. The countryside was beautiful and peaceful, exactly as I saw it a quarter of a century ago almost to the day. Nor did I feel any change in myself or in my love for H. V. . . .

I found some ten or twelve forget-me-nots in bloom. One of the Gwynne-Holford graves had taken the hint, and carried it out in a huge blue border of them. The grave (H. V.'s) is in so dark a corner they can't thrive very abundantly. I believe lilies of the valley might do better.

The fencing wants to be repainted dark green. I should love to do that, but must consult you when we meet. The shed is not so very unsightly, and ivy is fast making it less so. The tomb is sinking slightly on one side. It looks as though pilgrims had begun to go there, for inside the rings is quite a trodden-looking path. The yew tree should also be cleared of dead twigs, and its ivy destroyed.

Some day I must see it all again. . . .

To The Rev. A. F. Day, S. J.

LLANOVER HOUSE, ABERGAVENNY, S. WALES,
July 3, 1920.

DEAREST FATHER,—. . . We leave this big peaceful place on the 15th, for somewhere or other in the vicinity, as the workmen are coming in. Grace wants to be near the library, while her catalogue is being printed; and any locality not townish would suit me. I am negotiating for a slightly tumbledown but picturesque house, nicely furnished, at the outskirts of Aberg'enny, with a view of the mountains, which was once part of the ancient Priory of the Benedictines. Our devoted factotum, Annie Overton, stands ready to fly to our corporate bosom the moment we move. Then (what do you think?) I am to have Mrs. Mills's sweet house at Chipping Campden while she and Muriel are in Italy: which will be between Oct. and March. I shall very particularly like it, because I want a base in Oxon or Glos. for a thorough house-hunt. This no-roof-of-one's-own is getting desperate; and the big warehouse rental is always rolling up! But I have very, very much to be thankful for. *Imprimis*, admirable good health has for a long time blessed both Grace and me . . .

I thought of you, so I did, when I had to *sit* through raggedly sung hymns at Benediction in St. Aloysius. Dead, dead, dead . . . shall these dry bones live? The O. S. B. Pastor here is a real one: endlessly energetic, vigilant and apostolic: Fr. Hilary Willson. A bit of an antiquary, with not a gleam of humour. Lastly, with my best love, and a suggestion: Will you come to Abergavenny this summer and look in upon an aging but fightful friend? *"Some"* welcome, if you only will! Dinna forget to pray for your same.

L. I. G.

To Miss Shaughnessy

HILLGROVE, CLYTHA, NEAR ABERGAVENNY, SO. WALES,
29 July, 1920.

DEAR MISS SHAUGHNESSY,—It would give me true pleasure to help you out, but your scheme deals with the very thing I know least about: modern fiction. An English friend of mine who happens to be here, and knows his ground, says you will hardly be able to find short stories which combine true Catholic atmosphere and true literary value! You might do well to go over the borderline a little, and take in some things more like essays than fiction: as this would would allow a choice from the exquisite work of Mgr. Bickerstaffe-Drew (*Grace-church Papers*) and of Agnes Repplier (say a character sketch from *Convent Days*). Of course you have Mgr. Benson; Enid Dinnis, a valuable new Catholic writer; Miss G. V. Christmas; Fr. David Bearne, S. J.; Fr. Garrold; (*The Man's Hands,* etc.) and a convert writing since 1912 in *The Month,* who may or may not have published a book of her short stories, Mary Samuel Daniel. These are all I can think of apart from a forgotten American author, Mary Agnes Tincker, whose later books were "off the track," but whose volume entitled *The Winged Word* has some beautifully written things in it, two at least very poignantly Catholic. Have you looked over the list of the

(English) Catholic Truth Society? And there is the ever-charming Katharine Tynan Hinkson, who has done some Catholic short stories, though not many. . . .

Forgive so sketchy a letter,—the best I can do. I am working at top speed (in a little house among the hills, taken for two months) on a two-volume anthology and its endless annotation, which is occupying every ounce of my energy and every moment of my time. Please tell Fr. Earls, with affectionate best wishes, that my collaborator is Fr. Geoffrey Bliss, S. J., an old friend of ours, and that the opus is to be called *Recusant Poets*. . . .

Yours sincerely,
LOUISE I. GUINEY.

THE END